Creating a Photo Book for Seniors

WITHDRAWN

Studio Visual Steps

Creating a Photo Book
for Seniors

Everything you need to create a professionally printed photo book

www.visualsteps.com

This book has been written using the Visual Steps™ method.
Cover design by Studio Willemien Haagsma bNO

© 2011 Visual Steps
Edited by Jolanda Ligthart, Rilana Groot and Mara Kok
Translated by Chris Hollingsworth, *1st Resources* and Irene Venditti, *i-write* translation services.
Printed in Canada.

First printing: December 2011
ISBN 978 90 5905 247 5

Resources used: Some of the computer terms and definitions seen here in this book have been taken from descriptions found online at the Windows Help and Support website.

Do you have questions or suggestions?
E-mail: info@visualsteps.com

Would you like more information?
www.visualsteps.com

Website for this book:
www.visualsteps.com/photobook
Here you can register your book.

Register your book
We will keep you aware of any important changes that are necessary to you as a user of the book. You can also take advantage of our periodic newsletter informing you of our product releases, company news, tips & tricks, special offers, free guides, etcetera.

Table of Contents

Appendices

Foreword

Dear readers,

In this book you will find countless ideas to help get you started with your own photo book. For example a vacation book or travelogue, a chronicle of a baby's first year, a wedding or an autobiography. Using free online photo book software you can layout your story with text and embellish it further with photos and other graphical elements. Print services available from the photo book provider ensure that your photo book is carefully printed and professionally bound.

This book will show you how to work with the photo book software and offers many ideas and practical tips for writing text. You will also learn step by step how to transfer photos from your digital camera to your computer and how to scan older, printed photos.

Telling your own personal story in a unique book format has never been so easy!

Tip! This title would make an excellent gift for someone you know, to encourage him or her to write their own story. Perhaps, your father, mother, grandmother or grandfather, for instance.

We hope you enjoy this inspiring book!

Yvette Huijsman

P.S. We welcome all comments and suggestions regarding this book.
Our e-mail address is: info@visualsteps.com

Visual Steps Newsletter

All Visual Steps books follow the same methodology: clear and concise step-by-step instructions with screen shots to demonstrate each task. A complete list of all our books can be found on our website **www.visualsteps.com** You can also sign up to receive our **free Visual Steps Newsletter**.

In this Newsletter you will receive periodic information by e-mail regarding:
- the latest titles and previously released books;
- special offers, supplemental chapters, tips and free informative booklets.
Also, our Newsletter subscribers may download any of the documents listed on the web pages **www.visualsteps.com/info_downloads**

When you subscribe to our Newsletter you can be assured that we will never use your e-mail address for any purpose other than sending you the information as previously described. We will not share this address with any third-party. Each Newsletter also contains a one-click link to unsubscribe.

Introduction to Visual Steps™

The Visual Steps handbooks and manuals are the best instructional materials available for learning how to work with computers and computer programs. Nowhere else will you find better support for getting to know the computer, the iPad, the Internet, *Windows* or related software.

Properties of the Visual Steps books:
- **Comprehensible contents**
  Addresses the needs of the beginner or intermediate computer user for a manual written in simple, straight-forward English.
- **Clear structure**
  Precise, easy to follow instructions. The material is broken down into small enough segments to allow for easy absorption.
- **Screen shots of every step**
  Quickly compare what you see on your own computer screen with the screen shots in the book. Pointers and tips guide you when new windows are opened so you always know what to do next.
- **Get started right away**
  All you have to do is switch on your computer, place the book next to your keyboard, and begin at once.

In short, I believe these manuals will be excellent guides for you.

dr. H. van der Meij

Faculty of Applied Education, Department of Instruction Technology, University of Twente, the Netherlands

Register Your Book

When you can register your book, you will be kept informed of any important changes that are necessary to you as a user of the book. You can also take advantage of our periodic Newsletter informing you of our product releases, company news, tips & tricks, special offers, etcetera.

What You Will Need

In order to work through this book, you will need a number of things on your computer:

Several photo book providers require that you first download and install their photo book software before you can begin compiling your photo book. Other providers allow you to work directly online. In chapter 2 of this book you can read a summary of the options available by several well-known photo book providers. This will help you decide which photo book software to use. In chapter 3 we cover the photo book software from *Mixbook*. If you visit the website accompanying this book, you can download an extra chapter which covers the software from *Picaboo*.

This book has been made for computers running *Windows 7*, *Vista* or *XP*.
A high-speed Internet access (DSL or cable) is desirable for downloading the photo book software and uploading your completed photo book so that you can use the print services from your photo book provider. It is also handy when uploading your photos for the online versions of photo book software, such as *Mixbook*.

How to Use This Book

This book has been written using the Visual Steps™ method. You can work through this book independently at your own pace.

In this Visual Steps™ book, you will see various icons. This is what they mean:

Techniques
These icons indicate an action to be carried out:

 The mouse icon means you should do something with the mouse.

 The keyboard icon means you should type something on the keyboard.

 The hand icon means you should do something else, for example insert a CD-ROM in the computer. It is also used to remind you of something you have learned before.

In addition to these icons, in some areas of this book *extra assistance* is provided to help you successfully work through each chapter.

Help
These icons indicate that extra help is available:

 The arrow icon warns you about something.

 The bandage icon will help you if something has gone wrong.

 Have you forgotten how to do something? The number next to the footsteps tells you where to look it up at the end of the book in the appendix *How Do I Do That Again?*

In separate boxes you will find tips or additional, background information.

Extra information
Information boxes are denoted by these icons:

 The book icon gives you extra background information that you can read at your convenience. This extra information is not necessary for working through the book.

 The light bulb icon indicates an extra tip for using the program.

Prior Computer Experience

If you want to use this book, you will need some basic computer skills. If you do not have these skills, it is a good idea to read one of the following books first:

Windows 7 for SENIORS - ISBN 978 90 5905 126 3
Windows Vista for SENIORS - ISBN 978 90 5905 274 1
Windows XP for SENIORS - ISBN 978 90 5905 044 0

Website

On the website that accompanies this book, **www.visualsteps.com/photobook**, you will find further information. This website will also keep you informed of any errata, recent updates or other changes you need to be aware of, as a user of the book.
Don't forget to visit our website **www.visualsteps.com** from time to time to read about new books and other useful information such as handy computer tips, frequently asked questions and informative booklets.

Test Your Knowledge

Have you finished reading this book? Then test your knowledge with a test. Visit the website: **www.ccforseniors.com**

This multiple-choice test will tell you how good your computer knowledge is. If you pass the test, you will receive your free *Computer Certificate* by e-mail.

For Teachers

This book is designed as a self-study guide. It is also well suited for use in a group or a classroom setting. For this purpose, we offer a free teacher's manual containing information about how to prepare for the course (including didactic teaching methods) and testing materials. You can download this teacher's manual (PDF file) from the website which accompanies this book: **www.visualsteps.com/protect**

The Screen Shots

The screen shots in this book were made on a computer running *Windows 7 Ultimate* edition. The screen shots used in this book indicate which button, folder, file or hyperlink you need to click on your computer screen. In the instruction text (in **bold** letters) you will see a small image of the item you need to click. The black line will point you to the right place on your screen.

The small screen shots that are printed in this book are not meant to be completely legible all the time. This is not necessary, as you will see these images on your own computer screen in real size and fully legible.

Here you see an example of an instruction text and a screen shot. The black line indicates where to find this item on your own computer screen:

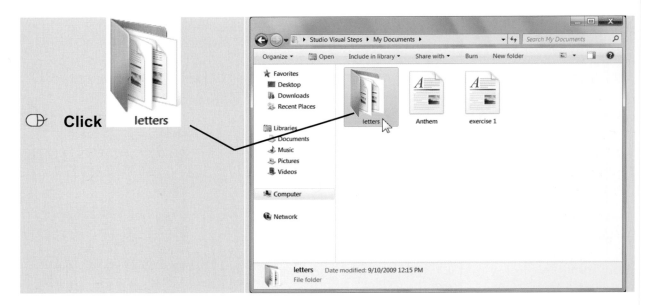

Sometimes the screen shot shows only a portion of a window. Here is an example:

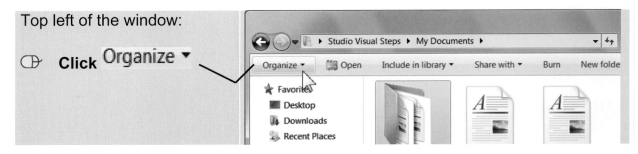

It really will **not be necessary** for you to read all the information in the screen shots in this book. Always use the screen shots in combination with the image you see on your own computer screen.

1. Introduction

Have you ever wanted to write a book about some of your own personal experiences? For instance, the story of your childhood, your son or daughter's wedding, your family history, challenges you have had and how you overcame them, or even an account of a fabulous trip you once made. But where do you start? What type of format should you choose? How do you get your book printed? You will find answers to these and many other questions in this book!

You will find countless ideas for writing stories about a multitude of different topics. One of these ideas is bound to get you inspired and motivate you to start creating your own book. There are tips on how to collect information, how to layout your story and various ideas for composition.

Once you have the main part of your story ready, you can start building your book. For this, you can use the software provided by various websites who offer online photo books. Most of the photo books made with these providers will contain photos and include a few titles and captions here and there. But some of the photo book providers offer many additional options for adding and formatting text. You can use a photo book to tell your own personal story or document an event and embellish it further by adding photos and other graphical elements.

This book will introduce you to a number of online photo book providers. This will help you to determine which one is best suited for your own book project. We also cover the software which is used to compile your book. You will learn how to add photos and background images, and how to format text. With so many examples in this book, you will never run short of inspiration. You can view larger renderings of the examples by visiting the website that accompanies this book: **www.visualsteps.com/photobook**

In the following section you can read about how this book is structured. A short description is given for each chapter. You can skip right to the chapter that interests you.

Chapter 2 Overview of Providers

In this chapter, we compare five providers of online photo book software. We have selected these five suppliers primarily on the basis of their user-friendly software.

The information in this chapter allows you to compare the options available in these programs, without having to try out all the software programs yourself.

To make it even easier for you, at the end of this chapter we include a brief summary of the results.

Chapter 3 Working with Mixbook

In this chapter you will learn how to use the *Mixbook* album software. With *Mixbook*, you can easily add photos and text to your photo book.

You will learn the basic operations such as adding photos and how to move and re-size them. You will also learn how to use the photo editing features. Next you will learn how to add text and apply text formatting. For further embellishment, you can add backgrounds, utilize templates, or select among a wide variety of photo frames, clip art or stickers.

 Please note!

If you prefer to use the *Picaboo* album software, you can download a different version of this chapter, by visiting the website that goes with this book: **www.visualsteps.com/photobook** On the website, look for the bonus chapter *Working with Picaboo*. You can open and print this PDF file with the free *Adobe Reader* program. If you do not yet have *Adobe Reader*, browse to **www.visualsteps.com/adobereader** and read how to download and install this program.

Chapter 4 Writing Tips

In this chapter you will find a number of tips to help you get started writing your own story. You will also learn how to avoid some well-known 'writers' pitfalls'.

This chapter will be your source of inspiration. There are many ideas you can use for your own story. You can also view examples of story albums that have already been made covering a number of different topics.

Chapter 5 Formatting Tips

The software that you use to build your photo book, offers many possibilities for formatting and editing. By choosing a specific layout, you can influence the 'look-and-feel' and character of a page. In this chapter you will find various examples of different templates. You will also learn how to construct text that is compelling and worthwhile reading.

You can of course select a different layout for each individual page. But by sticking to an identical format for every page, your album becomes more of a unified entity.
In this chapter you will learn how to turn your text into a coherent story.

Chapter 6 Collecting Photos

In this chapter you can read how to organize the photos that will be used in your photo book. If your photos are stored on your computer, you can collect them and save them in a separate folder designated for your photo book. If there are photos stored on your camera's memory card, you can copy them as well to this folder. You can also scan photos from old photo albums, and add them to your photo book.

In the following chapters, you will find many interesting tips and ideas for creating a photo book of your own.

Chapter 7 Create a Vacation Photo Book

For a great many people, the times spent around the vacations are the highlight of the year. Are you someone who looks forward to your vacation, months in advance? And do you like reminiscing and remembering your vacations afterwards? In this case, creating a photo book about some of your vacation experiences may be just the right thing for you!
In this type of album you can combine the prettiest vacation photos with your own personal story. You will find many ideas in this chapter, for the contents of your story, as well as the formatting of your album.

Chapter 8 Create a Wedding Day Book

A wedding day can generate some of the most meaningful moments in one's life. Perhaps you would like to create a story album about your son or daughter's wedding or that of a grandchild, niece or nephew. In this way, you can keep the memories of this beautiful day alive and share them with others. In this chapter you will find many ideas for creating a wedding day story album. We also provide a number of examples of wedding photo album pages, created using the album software from several different providers.

Chapter 9 Tell Your Life Story

If your children or grandchildren are always asking about things that happened to you in the past, it might be a great idea to create a story album about your own life or a particular episode in your life. The story album is a fun way of telling your children and grandchildren about your own experiences. This chapter will give many tips, ideas and examples of album pages, created by using the album software from several different providers.

Chapter 10 Write about a Baby's First Year

You can also use the album software to compile a baby book. In a story album you can document the changes that have occurred in your baby's first year and include photos you have taken. You can make this as extensive as you want: short captions to go with the photos, or longer stories recording each new phase in depth. This way, your story album becomes more expansive and meaningful than the traditional baby book.

This chapter provides a multitude of different ideas for the contents and formatting of a baby book. There are also various examples of album pages, created by using the album software from several different providers.

Other Ideas for Creating Photo Books

In chapters 7 through 10 of this book you will find other examples of photo books. You may already have an idea yourself for making a photo book. The possibilities are endless. Here are some more suggestions:

- A family cookbook
- Family pets
- First day at school
- Farewell to elementary school
- Graduation from middle school, high school
- High school dances; the Christmas ball, prom, etcetera
- College or university memories and experiences
- Fraternity, sorority or other club activity experiences
- A farewell party for a colleague
- A celebration event for an achievement or milestone reached (25 years worked, a promotion, a certification)
- A marriage anniversary
- Family reunion
- Affiliation with a sport, your team's games, events
- A story about your volunteer work
- A story about your hobby
- A school project
- A story about your neighborhood
- Moving into to a new house or a new neighborhood
- Redecorating, adding on, or rebuilding your home
- Putting in a garden for the first time, adding a vegetable or flower garden
- Documenting a yearly event, an annual parade, barbecue or picnic
- Halloween
- Thanksgiving
- Christmas / Boxing Day

2. Overview of Photo Book Providers

In the last few years, digital storytelling software has become immensely popular. The old way of ordering prints of your photos and then gluing them one by one by hand into a photo album seems to be dying out. This is not surprising, when you see all the features that have become available in various online software programs. You can create a photo book that is truly unique and special. For example, you can use different background images, apply templates, add text and frame your photos in a variety of ways. In a matter of minutes you can create a professional looking photo book, which you will be proud to present to your family and friends.

As more and more companies enter the market in online photo book software, it may seem difficult to find the right provider best suited for the type of book you want to make. Some of the software providers do not allow you to add both photos and text, or the text editing options are too limited. Other providers may limit the number of pages, or have no options for photo editing.

In this chapter we compare five online photo book providers. They all offer software that is easy to use (our primary requirement) and feature many additional options. You can read about what these five programs have to offer, without having to actually use the software on your own. At the end of this chapter we provide a full summary of all the results.

In this chapter you can read about:

- the suppliers' names and website addresses;
- which programs can be used online and/or offline;
- options for adding pages and designing the cover;
- options for using background images;
- options for text editing;
- options for adding and modifying text boxes;
- options for using frames, templates and clip art;
- options for alignment of the objects to a grid;
- options for photo editing;
- options for moving pages;
- a summary of the results.

2.1 Names and Web Addresses

Here you see an overview of the photo book providers we are going to discuss and compare along with their website address. All of these providers allow online purchasing, and they will ship the photo books to your home address.

Name:	Website:
	www.mixbook.com
	www.mypublisher.com
	www.shutterfly.com
	www.blurb.com
	www.picaboo.com

 Please note!

Prices may differ between the various photo books and the type of albums that are on offer. Also the shipping costs to Australia, the United Kingdom or other countries, will be higher. For the most current price information, please consult the individual provider's website.

 Please note!

There are many other providers of online photo books, besides the ones that are covered in this chapter. We have selected these five particular providers not only because their software is easy to use, but they also provide a number of extra features and include additional editing options for creating photo books.

2.2 Work Online or Offline

Some online photo book providers enable you to compile your photo book while you work online. This means that you must upload all of the photos you plan to use first. After you have done this, you can begin creating your photo book on the provider's website. You will need a continuous connection with the Internet, while you are compiling the book.

Other providers will allow you to work offline. You can download the album software from their website and install it onto your computer. While you are creating your photo book, you do not need to be connected to the Internet. You can add photos from the various folders on your computer. When you have finished and are ready to order and pay for the photo book, you will need to connect to the Internet again.

Name:	Online or offline	Comment:
Mixbook	online	
MyPublisher	offline	
Shutterfly	online	
Blurb	online and offline	The online version of the software is much more limited than the offline version. In this chapter we will discuss the offline version, called *Blurb BookSmart*.
Picaboo	offline	

2.3 Number of Pages

All photo book providers offer a choice of different photo book sizes. In order to be able to make an adequate comparison, we have chosen a standard photo book size of approximately 8 x 11 inches, with a hard cover. For this type of photo book, the number of pages offered is more or less the same. Almost all providers offer a book of about 100 pages, *Blurb* even offers 440 pages. You can add extra pages to the photo book, 1 or 2 pages at a time.

Name:	Minimum number of pages:	Add extra pages per:	Maximum number of pages:
Mixbook	20	2	99
MyPublisher	20	2	100
Shutterfly	20	1	101
Blurb	20	2	440
Picaboo	10	1	160*

* for standard paper. For lay-flat paper 90 pages maximum. See the Picaboo website.

2.4 The Cover

All of the providers allow you to print a cover with one or more of your own photos, including text, if you wish. Each provider also offers a large selection of colors to choose from for the cover.

Each provider allows the possibility of using a photo as a background for the cover, but not all providers will let you add an additional photo above that, for example, by inserting it in an overlaying photo box.

It is also possible to place a photo in a photo box and use colors or patterns as a background.

Name:	Photo in background and photo overlaying, in photo box	Color or pattern
Mixbook	yes	both
MyPublisher	yes	color
Shutterfly	no	both
Blurb	yes	color
Picaboo	yes	both

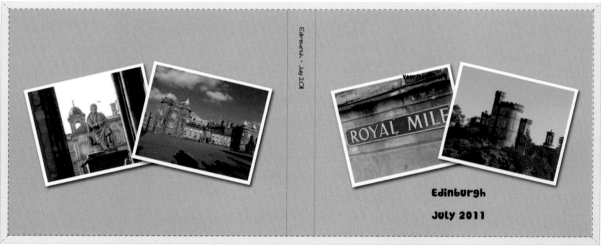

Example of a cover | Program: Picaboo | Background color: EBECB1

2.5 Using Background Images

You can achieve a nice effect, by filling the pages in your photo book with a background image. Most of the programs will allow you to use a background color, or one of the standard patterns that are included. Often, these patterns are arranged by their themes, such as holidays, travel, wedding, summer, winter, etcetera.

Name:	Colors	Patterns	Theme
Mixbook	yes	yes	yes
MyPublisher	yes	no	no
Shutterfly	yes	yes	yes
Blurb	yes	yes	no
Picaboo	yes	yes	yes

Program:
Mixbook

Standard background

Program:
Picaboo

Standard background
photo spread across
two pages

You can achieve another nice effect by using your own photo as a background image. In some of the programs you can blur the background image and/or spread it across two pages.

Name:	Own photo as background?	Render background transparent?	Background across two pages?	Standard backgrounds available?
Mixbook	yes	yes	yes	yes
MyPublisher	yes	yes	no	yes
Shutterfly	yes	yes	no	yes
Blurb	yes	no	no	yes
Picaboo	yes	yes	yes, but only with own photo	yes

Program: Shutterfly

Your own photo as background, 40% transparent

Standard frame

2.6 Using a Photo

All five programs will let you insert images directly from your computer. Some of the programs allow you to integrate photos from photo websites and social network sites.

Name:	Sites
Mixbook	Facebook, Flickr, Photobucket, SmugMug and Picasa
MyPublisher	None
Shutterfly	Facebook
Blurb	Flickr, SmugMug, Picasa, Photobucket
Picaboo	Facebook, Flickr

2.7 Editing Text

If you want to add text to a photo book, it is useful if the program offers extended options for text editing. Most programs will allow you to edit the text directly in the text box. This way, you will immediately see what the text in the text box looks like. Shutterfly is the only program with a separate editor for editing the text in a text box.

All five programs offer a sufficient choice of fonts. But some programs will not allow you to format various parts of a text in a different way, within the same text box. This means for example, that if you want your title to appear in a larger font, you will need to add an extra text box for it.

Name:	Edit text in text box or in editor?	Available fonts	Different formatting for parts of text within text box?
Mixbook	text box	40	yes
MyPublisher	text box	more than 300 fonts	yes
Shutterfly	editor	55 fonts	no
Blurb	text box	more than 300 fonts	yes
Picaboo	text box	40 fonts, more can be installed	no

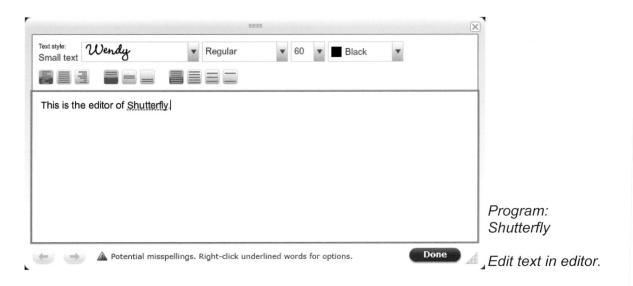

Program:
Shutterfly

Edit text in editor.

2.8 Adding and Editing Text Boxes

If you are creating a photo book with a large amount of text, you will want to be able to add, enlarge and shrink text boxes, without too much trouble. Adding a text box is easy, in all of the programs. Enlarging and shrinking a box is usually done by dragging the borders of the box. You can also move the entire text box and drag it to the desired location.

Name:	Easily add text boxes?	Easily move text boxes?	Enlarge/shrink text box
Mixbook	yes	yes	with corner and side handles
MyPublisher	yes	yes	with corner and side handles
Shutterfly	yes	yes	with corner and side handles
Blurb	fairly easy, done with edit layout	fairly easy, done with edit layout	with corner and side handles in Edit Layout window
Picaboo	yes	yes	with corner and side handles

This is how you enlarge or shrink a text or photo box in the *Picaboo* album software:

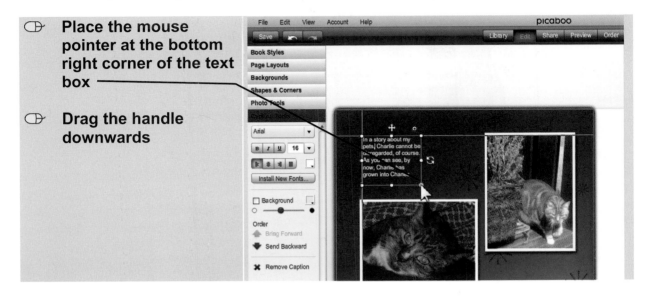

- **Place the mouse pointer at the bottom right corner of the text box**

- **Drag the handle downwards**

2.9 Working with Frames, Masks and Clip Art

You can enhance your photo book even further by adding frames, masks or stickers. A frame is a type of stylized border that surrounds a picture. Frames are available in a variety of styles and patterns. A mask is a creative way of cropping a photo. Some programs even offer stickers or other ornaments for decorating an album page.

Not all of the programs offer all of these features:

Name:	Frames available?	Masks/shapes available?	Stickers available?
Mixbook	yes	yes	yes
MyPublisher	no	no	no
Shutterfly	yes	no	yes
Blurb	yes	no	no, just small ornaments to put at the top and bottom of a page
Picaboo	yes	yes	yes, but you can only add these images to the corners of the photos

Program: Mixbook | Standard background across two pages | Left photo: mask applied | Right photo: two different frames used

Program: Shutterfly | Standard background applied to two pages | Various stickers added

2.10 Aligning to a Grid

While you are building a photo book with photo boxes and text boxes, it is very useful to be able to align these boxes to a grid. In this way, you can position the boxes to the exact same height, or make them equal in size. Some programs offer possibilities for aligning objects to a grid, but will not display this grid by default. Instead, you will sometimes see drawing aids (lines). Other programs will display the grid, but no drawing aids.

Name:	Grid displayed?	Drawing aids?
Mixbook	no	no
MyPublisher	not by default, but it can be set	no
Shutterfly	no	yes, only in Customize page window
Blurb	no, only in Edit Layout window	no
Picaboo	not by default, but it can be set	yes

Program:
Picaboo

Grid is displayed on the page

Drawing aids for moving, enlarging or shrinking photo and text boxes

2.11 Options for Photo Editing

Not all photos are perfect right from the start. It is very handy if the album software includes some basic photo editing features that will allow you to remove red eyes, crop photos or adjust the brightness or contrast. Sometimes there are additional options for applying special effects, such as rendering photos in a sepia tone or in black & white.

Name:	Remove red eyes	Crop	Brightness contrast saturation	Special effects
Mixbook	no	no, but possible by first zooming in and then moving the photo	yes	only gray scales and sepia
MyPublisher	yes	yes	no	yes, only black & white
Shutterfly	yes	yes	no	only black & white and blur
Blurb	no	no, but possible by first zooming in and then moving the photo	no	no
Picaboo	yes	no, but possible by first zooming in and then moving the photo	yes	only gray scales and sepia

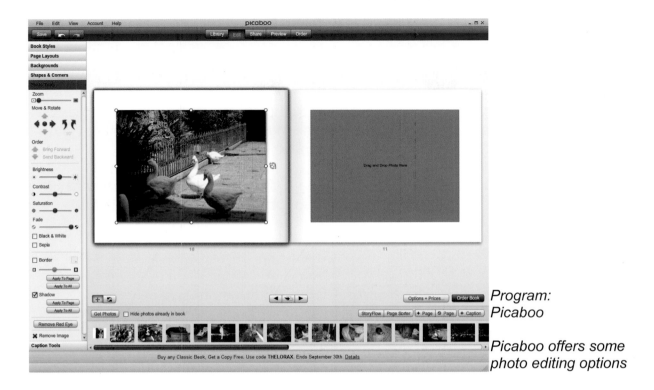

Program: Picaboo

Picaboo offers some photo editing options

2.12 Moving Pages

It often happens that while building your photo book, you decide to change the order of the pages. Almost all of the five programs have options for moving blank pages, as well as edited pages containing objects. Some programs allow you to position a photo across two pages; (a two-page spread) half of the photo will be printed on one page, and the other half on the other, adjacent page.

Name:	Move blank page	Move edited page	Two-page spread
Mixbook	yes	yes	yes
MyPublisher	no	yes	yes
Shutterfly	yes	yes	no
Blurb	yes	yes	no
Picaboo	yes	yes	no

2.13 Sharing a Photo Book

After you have created a photo book in *Picaboo*, you can share it with friends, by sending them an e-mail with a link to the photo book, or by using *Facebook*. *Mixbook* even allows you to collaborate the building of your photo book with friends or family. You send an e-mail invitation and ask them if they would like to help you compile the photo book. The final version can also be viewed by friends.

Name:	Collaborate with friends	Share finished version with friends
Mixbook	yes	yes
MyPublisher	no	no
Shutterfly	no	yes
Blurb	no	no
Picaboo	no	yes

2.14 Summary

In this table we have summarized all the results:

Name:	Mixbook	MyPublisher	Shutterfly	Blurb	Picaboo
Offline	no	yes	no	yes	yes
Pages minimum	20	20	20	20	10
Pages maximum	99	100	101	440	160
Extra pages per	2	2	1	2	1
Photo as background for cover and overlay photo box	yes	yes	no	yes	yes
Background color on cover	yes	yes	yes	yes	yes
Pattern on cover	yes	no	yes	no	yes
Patterns as background for pages	yes	no	yes	yes	yes
Themes available	yes	no	yes	no	yes
Own photo as background	yes	yes	yes	yes	yes
Transparent background	yes	yes	yes	no	yes
Background across two pages	yes	no	no	no	yes
Standard backgrounds	yes	yes	yes	yes	yes
Edit text in editor or in text box	text box	text box	editor	text box	text box

Name:	Mixbook	MyPublisher	Shutterfly	Blurb	Picaboo
Fonts	40	300+	55	300+	40
Different formatting in text box	yes	yes	no	yes	no
Easily add text boxes	yes	yes	yes	reasonably	yes
Easily move text boxes	yes	yes	yes	reasonably	yes
enlarge/shrink directly by dragging border	yes	yes	yes	yes*	yes
Frames	yes	no	yes	yes	yes
Masks	yes	no	no	no	yes
Stickers	yes	no	yes	yes*	yes*
Grid displayed	no	no*	no	no*	no*
Drawing aids for moving boxes	no	no	yes*	no	yes
Remove red eyes	no	yes	yes	no	yes
Crop	no*	yes	yes	no*	no*
Brightness, contrast, color	yes	no	no	no	yes
Special effects	yes*	yes*	yes*	no	yes*
Move blank pages	yes	no	yes	yes	yes
Move edited pages	yes	yes	yes	yes	yes

See the explanation in the relevant section

Based on these results, we have selected two software providers. In the following chapter you can read how to work with *Mixbook*. On the website that accompanies this book you can download the same chapter for the *Picaboo* program. See the next chapter for more information.

3. Working with Mixbook

In the previous chapter you have read about several providers that offer software for creating a photo book with text. In this chapter you will learn how to use the *Mixbook* photo book software.

Mixbook software is easy to use and offers a wide variety of layout options. You will quickly be able to add photos and text to your photo book. In this chapter we cover all the basic operations such as adding, moving, and resizing photos and adding and formatting text. You will also learn how to further embellish the book, by adding backgrounds, pre-designed templates and frames.

In this chapter you will learn how to:

- start *Mixbook*;
- select and open a photo book;
- add photos;
- resize and reposition photo boxes;
- use templates and frames;
- add backgrounds;
- add text boxes, resize and reposition them;
- add text to a text box and apply text formatting;
- copy text from a text editing program;
- add and delete pages;
- change the order of the pages;
- send your photo book to the print service and pay for it.

 Please note!

If you prefer to use an album software program other than *Mixbook*, you can visit the website that accompanies this book. You can download a different version of this chapter that covers the *Picaboo* software.

On **www.visualsteps.com/photobook** you will find the bonus chapter *Working with Picaboo*. You can open and print these PDF file with the free *Adobe Reader* program. If you do not have *Adobe Reader* yet, go to **www.visualsteps.coml/adobereader** and read how to download and install this program.

➥ Please note!

The *Mixbook* website and the software provided are continuously being improved and updated. This means that the windows, backgrounds or buttons that appear on your screen may look different from the screen shots in this book. If that is the case and it is a button you are looking for, take a good look around the web page and try to find a similar button.

If any major changes occur in the software, we will place a revised version of this chapter on the website accompanying this book. The website address is **www.visualsteps.com/photobook**

3.1 Starting Mixbook

The *Mixbook* website allows you to use their photo book software for free, no download is necessary. You can use the software to create and order a photo book. After you have paid for the photo book, you can have it sent to your home address or have it shipped anywhere else in the world.

This is how you start the *Mixbook* program:

☞ **Start** *Internet Explorer* 𝄞¹

☞ **Go to the www.mixbook.com webpage** 𝄞²

In order to create a photo book, you need to make an account:

☐ **Click** Signup

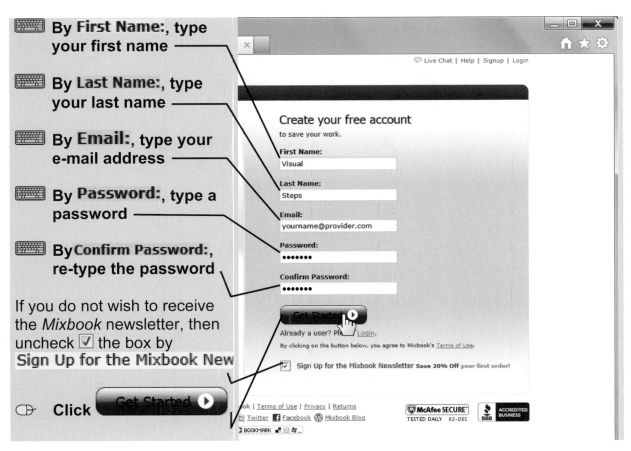

By **First Name:**, type your first name ⎯

By **Last Name:**, type your last name ⎯

By **Email:**, type your e-mail address ⎯

By **Password:**, type a password ⎯

By **Confirm Password:**, re-type the password

If you do not wish to receive the *Mixbook* newsletter, then uncheck ☑ the box by
Sign Up for the Mixbook New

Click **Get Started** ▶

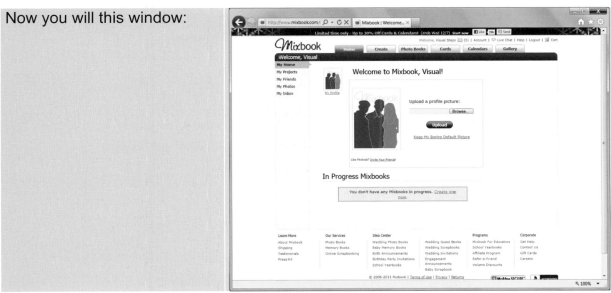

Now you will this window:

3.2 Creating a New Photo Book

You are going to create a new photo book. You can choose various types of photo books.

⏲ **Click** **Photo Books**

You will see the various types of photo books. In this example you choose the Classic landscape format of 11 x 8 inch:

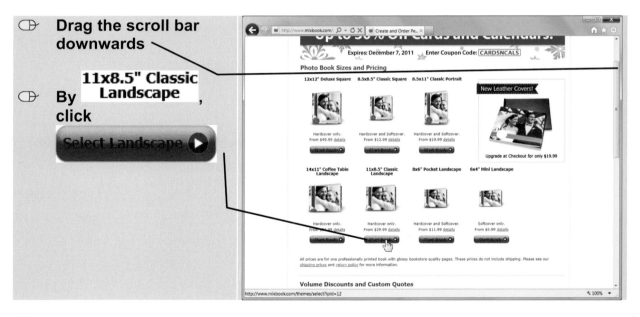

⏲ **Drag the scroll bar downwards**

⏲ **By** **11x8.5" Classic Landscape**, **click** **Select Landscape** ▶

🡆 Please note!

It is possible that the program offers different products than the ones you see in the picture above. And in the meantime, the pricing may have changed too. Be sure to visit the *Mixbook* website to find out the most current prices and special offers.

Mixbook lets you select a theme. This may be useful, but for now you are going to start by creating a blank photo book:

Click

I don't want to choose

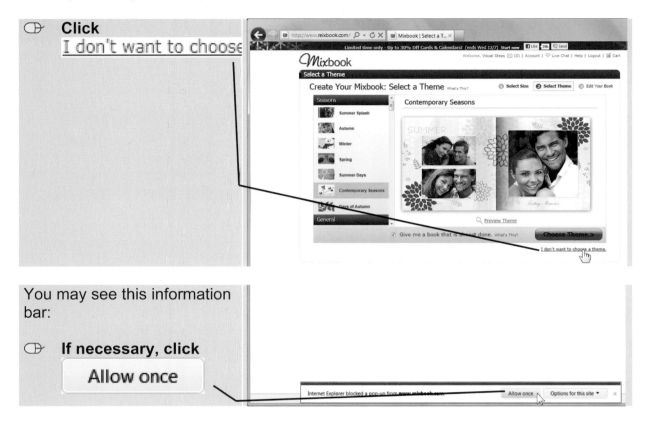

You may see this information bar:

If necessary, click

Allow once

Mixbook has an option for selecting photos for the photo book. But you are going to do this manually, so you can close this window now:

Click CLOSE ✕

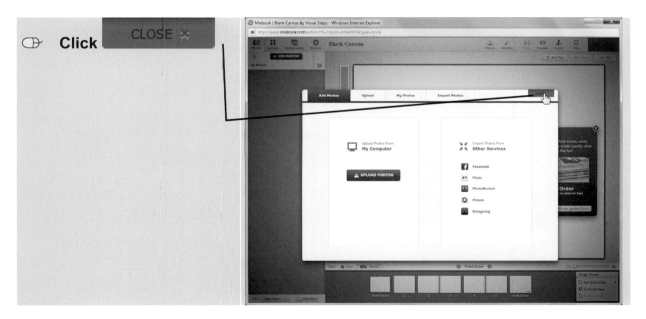

You will see another window open. You can close this window too:

Click ✕

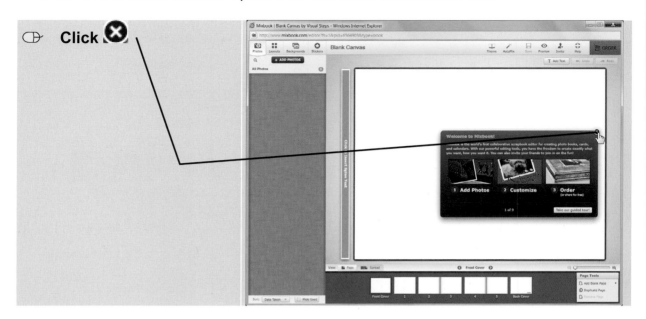

Now you will see the *Mixbook* workspace:

On the left-hand side you see the tab with which you can select photos: ————

Here you see the page you are editing. In this case you will see the front of the page: ┐

Here you can select the pages you want to edit: ——

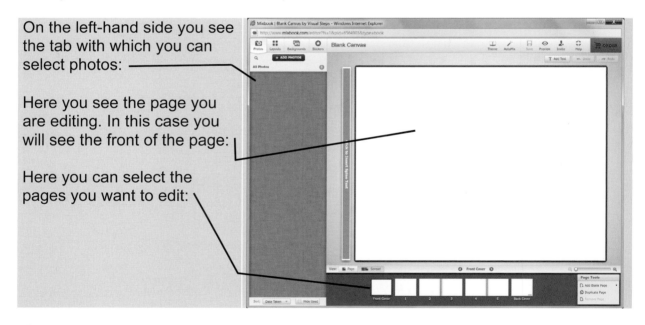

💡 Tip

Select a theme
In this example, we have not selected a theme. *Mixbook* offers a wide variety of themes which you can select before you start adding photos to the album. In the *Tips* section at the end of this chapter, you can find more information about themes.

3.3 Adding Photos

In *Mixbook* it is very easy to add photos to the photo book. You can try this now.

 Please note!

In this example we have used some sample photos, but you can use your own photos if you like.

If you do not have any photos stored on your computer, you can download the sample photos used in this chapter. Go to **www.visualsteps.com/photobook** There you will find the sample photos, including instructions for how to download them to the *(My) Pictures* folder on your computer.

The photos that are used in these examples are stored in the *(My) Pictures* folder, in the subfolder *Practice Files*. This is how you open the *(My) Pictures* folder:

In the left-hand side of the window:

☞ **Click** **+ ADD PHOTOS**

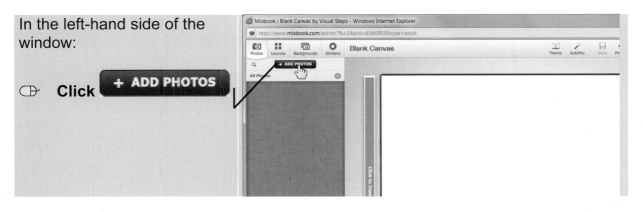

☞ **Click** **⬆ UPLOAD PHOTOS**

You will see the folder window:

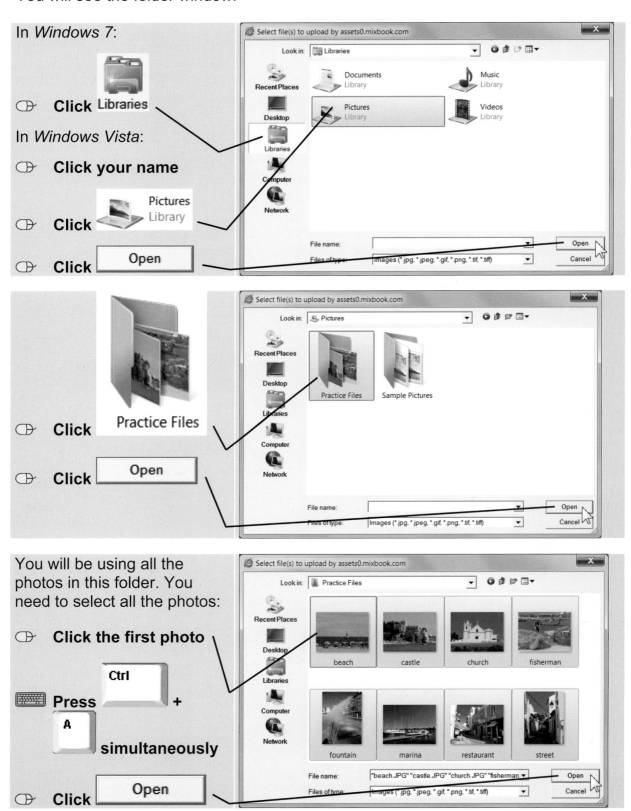

In *Windows 7*:

🖰 **Click** Libraries

In *Windows Vista*:

🖰 **Click your name**

🖰 **Click** Pictures Library

🖰 **Click** Open

🖰 **Click** Practice Files

🖰 **Click** Open

You will be using all the photos in this folder. You need to select all the photos:

🖰 **Click the first photo**

⌨ **Press** Ctrl + A **simultaneously**

🖰 **Click** Open

The photos will now be added: —————

This may take a while.

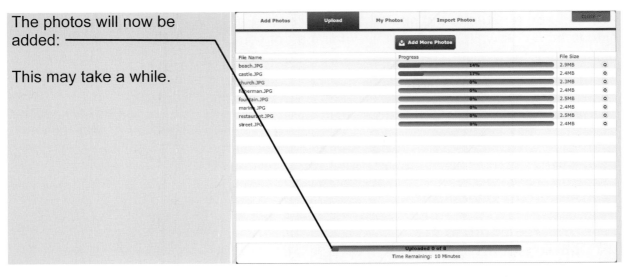

After all the photos have been added, you will see this message

Your photos are finished!.

Now you can close this window:

⊕ **Click** [CLOSE ✖]

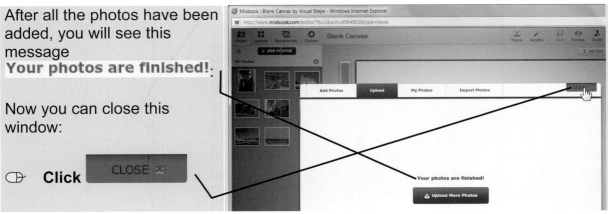

In the left-hand side of the work space you will see the thumbnail images of the sample photos:

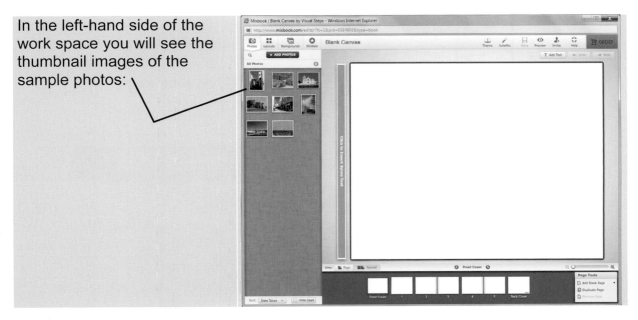

You can add a photo to the photo book by dragging a thumbnail from the left-hand side to the large white surface in the main part of your screen. This is how you add a photo to the front cover:

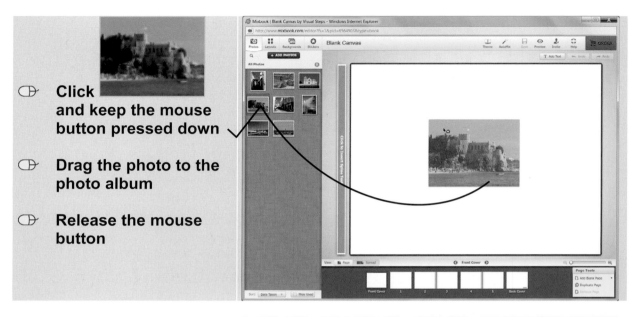

☞ **Click and keep the mouse button pressed down**

☞ **Drag the photo to the photo album**

☞ **Release the mouse button**

The photo has now been placed on the front cover:

Now you can continue with the next page in the album:

☞ **Click**

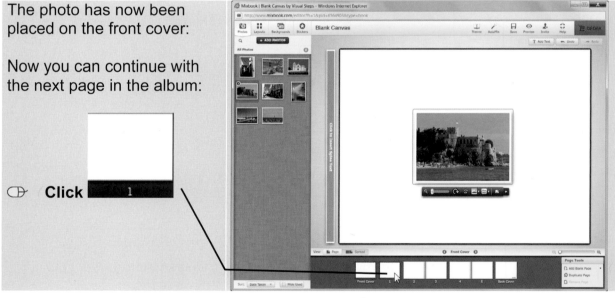

In many instances, the album software will not allow you to print a photo on the inside of the cover. This means you can only insert a photo onto a single page:

 Drag 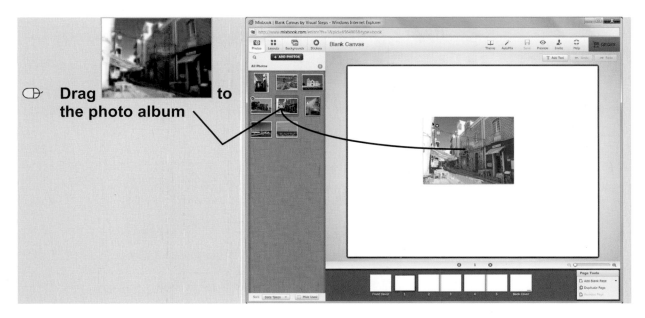 **to the photo album**

Now the first page has also been filled in:

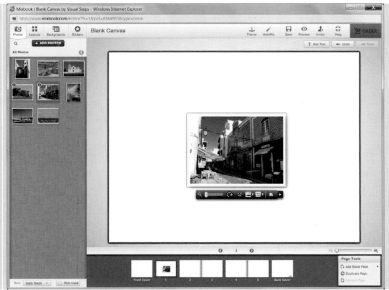

💡 Tip

Save your work in the meantime
If you do not have time to continue working on your photo book, you can save your work. In *section 3.15 Save Your Photo Book* you can read how to do this.

3.4 Selecting a Page Layout

Mixbook has not yet suggested a page layout. You can set this page layout separately, for each individual page. First, go to the next page of the photo book:

☞ **Click** ▶

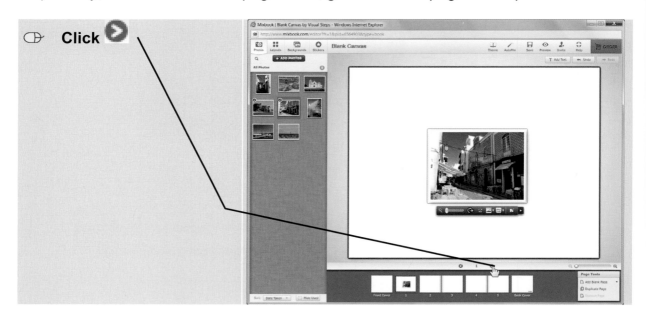

You will see pages 2 and 3. The left page has been selected. This is indicated by the orange border:

Now you are going to set the page layout for this page:

☞ **Click** Layouts

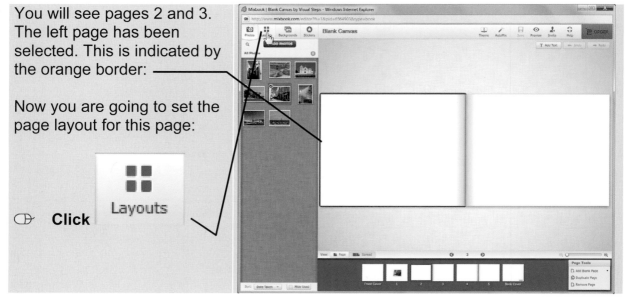

You are going to select a layout which includes two photos and a text box:

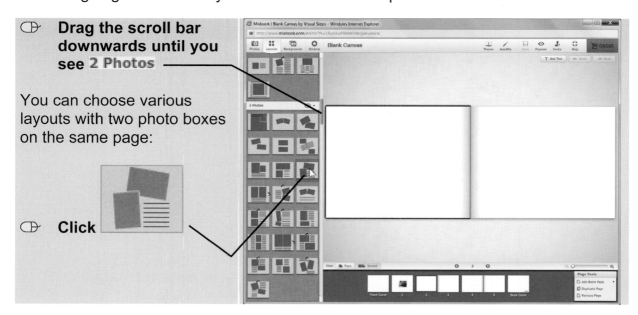

⮞ **Drag the scroll bar downwards until you see** 2 Photos

You can choose various layouts with two photo boxes on the same page:

⮞ **Click**

Now this layout will be applied to the selected page.

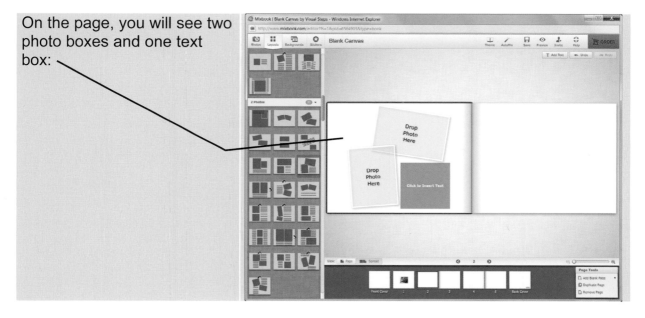

On the page, you will see two photo boxes and one text box:

Now you can fill the photo boxes with photos:

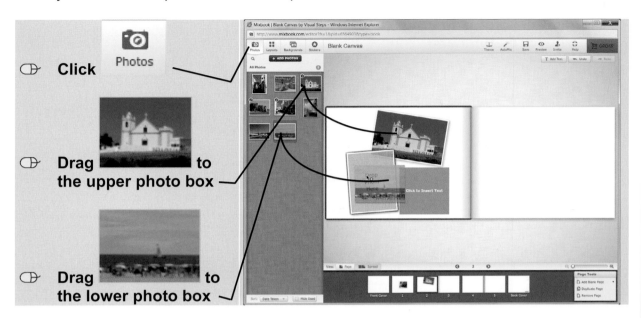

You are also going to insert a photo on page 3:

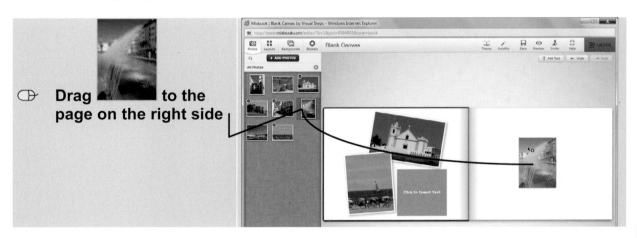

💡 Tip

Different photo
If you prefer to add a different photo to this photo box, you can drag a new photo across the old one and replace it.

3.5 Reducing or Enlarging Photo and Text Boxes

If you do not like the size of the photo and text boxes, you can modify them. This is how you reduce the photo on the right-hand page:

☞ **Click the photo**

☞ **Position the mouse pointer on the corner handle at the top left**

The pointer will turn into ⬉:

☞ **Drag the corner handle to the right and downwards**

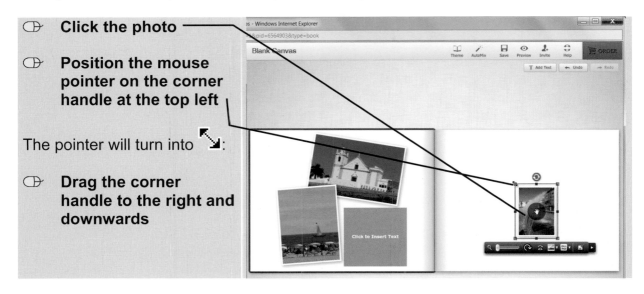

The photo box will be made smaller, while retaining the same height/width aspect ratio. If you start dragging from the corner of the frame, the aspect ratio of the photo will remain the same. If you start dragging at the middle of one of the sides, the photo will become narrower or wider.

Here is how to turn the photo box so that it will fit a landscape photo, rather than a portrait photo:

☞ **Click the photo to the right**

☞ **Position the mouse pointer on the top middle handle**

The pointer will turn into ⬌:

☞ **Drag the handle to the left**

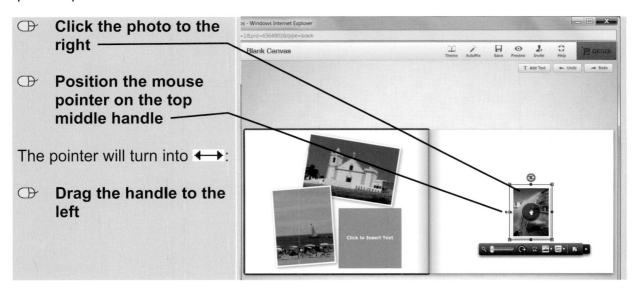

Now the fountain is rendered in landscape orientation:

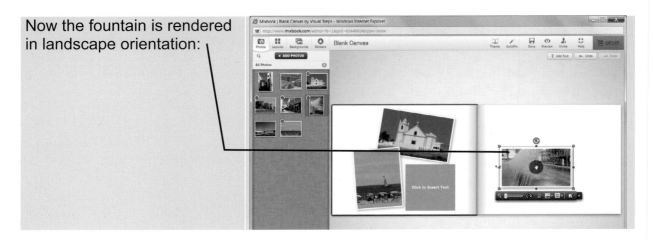

☞ **Enlarge or decrease the size of your photo as desired** ⁵

💡 **Tip**

Portrait photos
The standard page layouts include pages with photo boxes in both portrait and landscape orientation of the photos.

Now you are going to increase the size of the text box on the left page. This is done in the same manner as enlarging or decreasing a photo:

☞ **Click the text box on the left page**

☞ **Position the mouse pointer on the top middle handle**

The pointer will turn into ←→:

☞ **Drag the handle to the right**

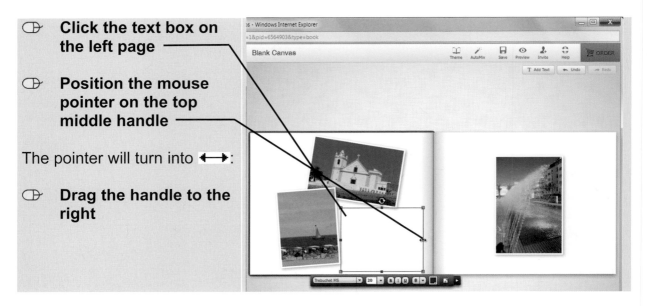

The text box partially covers the photos. You can remedy this by moving the photo.

3.6 Moving Photo and Text Boxes

You can move the photo and text boxes. This is how you move the photo on the left-hand page:

☞ **Click the photo at the bottom**

The pointer will turn into ✛ :

☞ **Drag the photo box to the left**

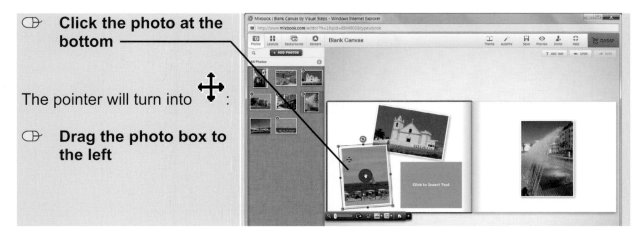

In the same way, you can move a text box.

3.7 Adding a Photo

If a page contains too few photo boxes, you can add an extra photo. The quickest way of doing this, is dragging the desired photo directly on to the page:

☞ **Drag [ ] to the page on the right side**

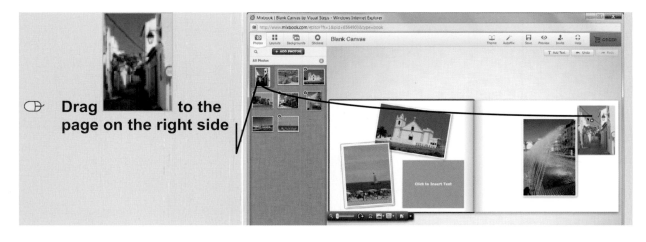

The photo has been placed on the page:

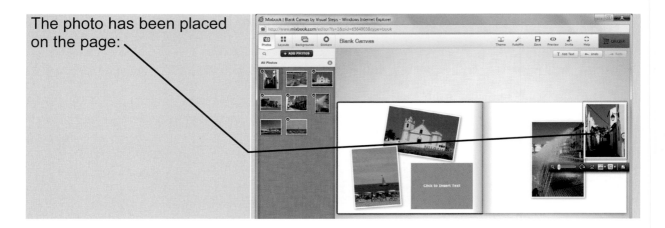

3.8 Deleting a Photo

You can delete any photo you no longer want to use. Like this:

On the right page:

◯▷ **Right-click the photo**

◯▷ **Click Delete Selection**

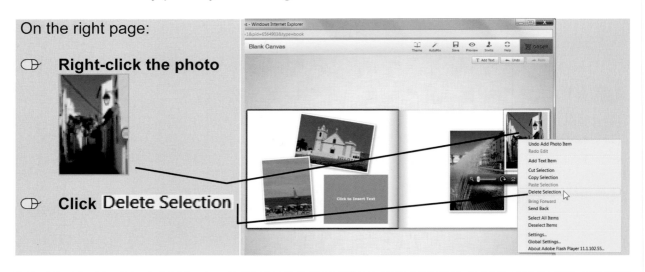

Now the photo has been removed:

3.9 Using Shapes

Mixbook contains many options for enhancing the pages in your book. Just try them:

☞ **Click the top photo on the left page**

☞ **Click**

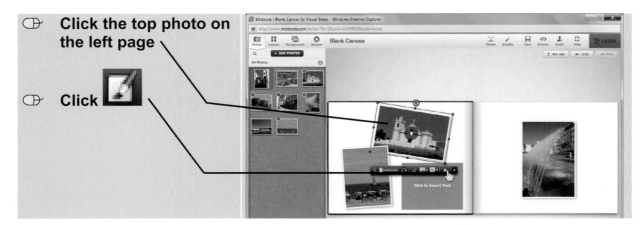

You will see a small window:

To change the shape of the figure into a circle/oval:

☞ **Click**

☞ **Click**

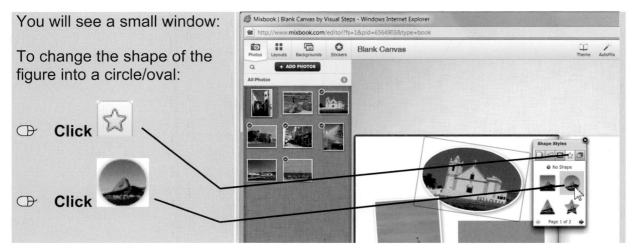

The shape will be applied to the photo.

☞ **Click a spot somewhere in the window**

You will see the result of the selected shape:

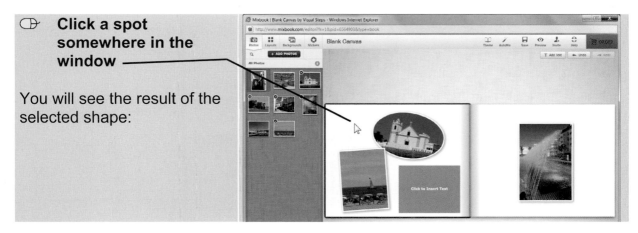

Tip

Delete a shape
If you decide not to use the shape after all, you can delete it again. This is how you do it:

↪ **Right-click the photo with the shape**
↪ **Click** Undo Style

3.10 Using Frames

Mixbook will add a white frame around your photo by default. You can change this frame:

↪ **Click the photo on the right page**

↪ **Click**

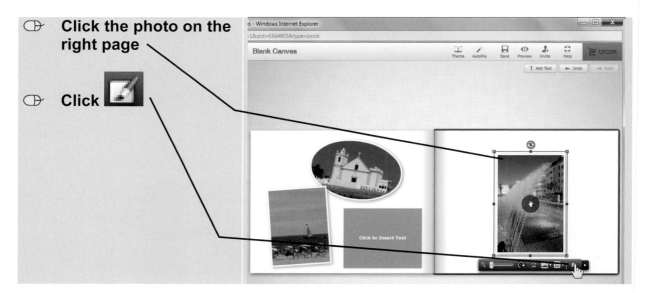

You are going to select a black frame:

↪ **Click**

↪ **Click**

↪ **Click**

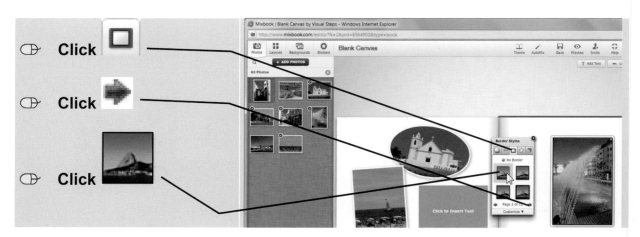

⏺ **Click next to the photo**

Now the frame has been
added to the photo:

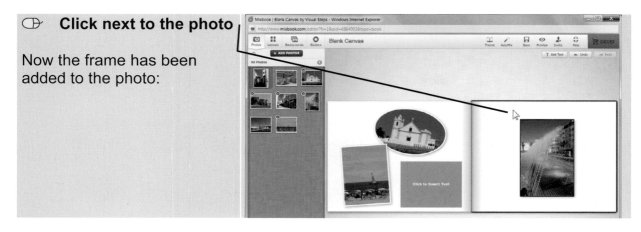

  Tip
Remove a frame
If, on second thought, you do not want to use the frame, you can delete it. This is
how you do it:

⏺ **Right-click the photo with the frame**
⏺ **Click Undo Border**

3.11 Adding a Background Color

You can make your photo book look even more professional by adding backgrounds
to the pages. Start by adding a simple colored background. Choose a color for the
background of the left page:

⏺ **Click the left page**

⏺ **Click** Backgrounds

⏺ **By** Background Color:,
  click ▪.

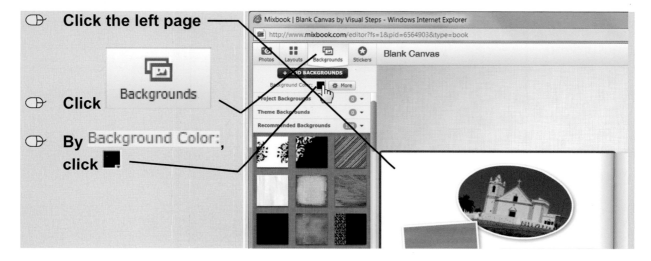

You will see a window with different colors:

☞ **Click** ☐

You can click a different color.

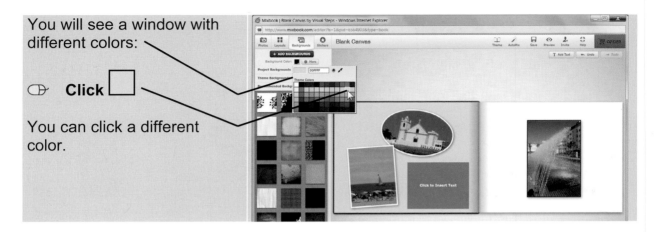

Now the background of the left page has become your chosen color.

3.12 Using a Background Image

Mixbook offers a large number of standard background images that you can use for your book:

In the left-hand side of the window:

☞ **Click** ☐

You can click a different background.

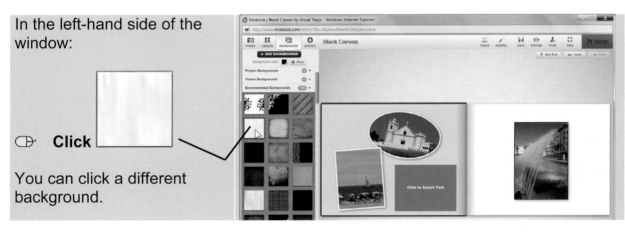

You will see that the background image has been applied to the left page and the bright blue color has disappeared:

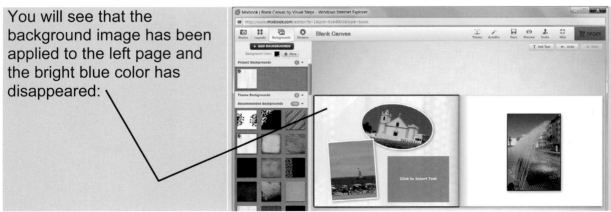

3.13 Use Your Own Photo as a Background

You can also use one of your own photos as a background. Try this out on the right page:

☞ **Click the right page**

☞ **Click**

+ ADD BACKGROUNDS

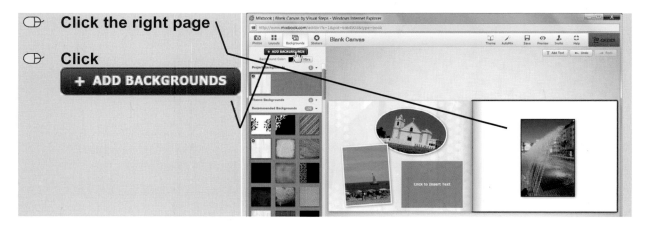

☞ **Click**

Upload Content

☞ **Click**

⬆ UPLOAD BACKGROUNDS

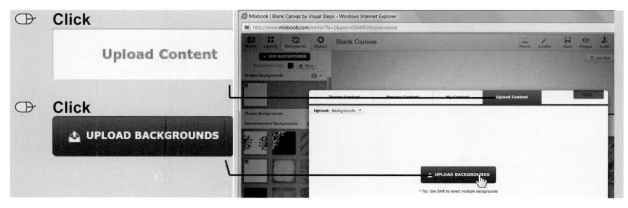

☞ **Open the *Practice Files* folder** ✌4

☞ **Click** (marina)

☞ **Click** **Open**

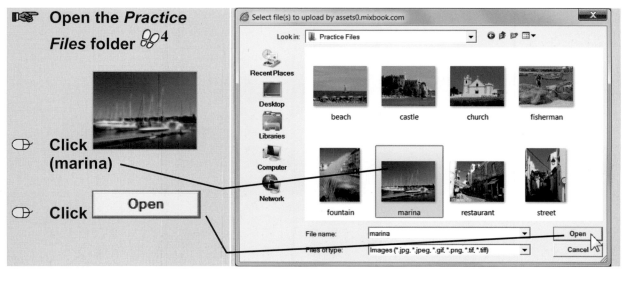

Now the photo will be added:

After the photo has been added, you will see this message
Your backgrounds are finished!:

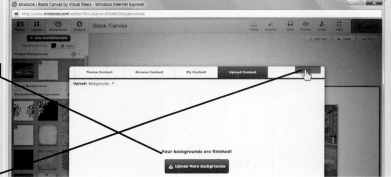

You can close this window:

👉 **Click** CLOSE ✖

In the left-hand side of the window:

👉 **Click**

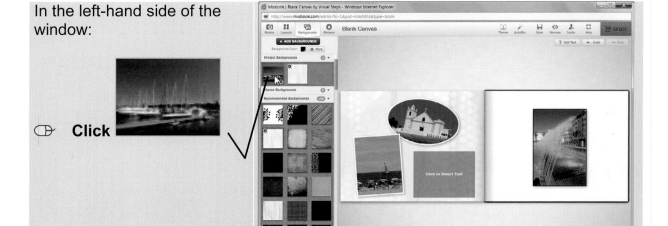

Now the photo will be
rendered as a background on
the selected page:

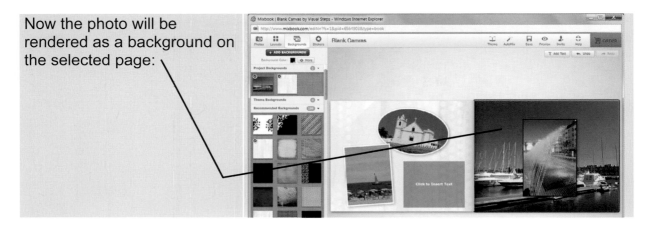

You can fade the background photo by modifying the degree of transparency:

☞ **Click** More

☞ **Drag the slider ○ by**
   Color Opacity: **to 54%**

3.14 Undo and Redo

If you decide not to use the background, you can undo the last operation:

☞ **Click** ← Undo

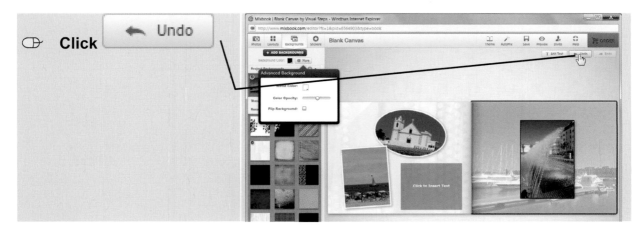

Now you will see the previous background again:

If you prefer to re-insert the photo as a background, you can redo the last operation:

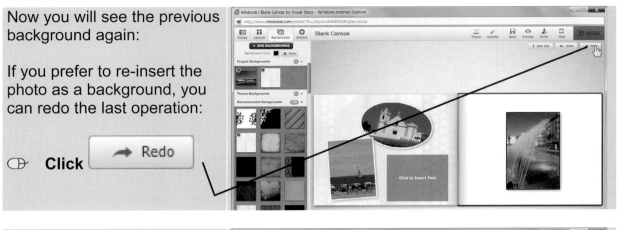

☞ **Click** [→ Redo]

Now the photo appears once more in the background:

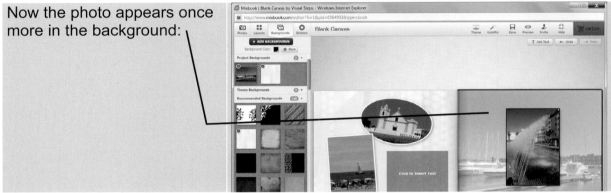

💡 **Tip**
Delete background
This is how to quickly delete the background of a page:

☞ **Right-click the background you want to remove**
☞ **Click** Undo Background Color

3.15 Save Your Photo Book

It is important to save the photo book you are editing at regular intervals. This will prevent you from accidentally losing the file. It is very simple to save your work:

☞ **Click** Save

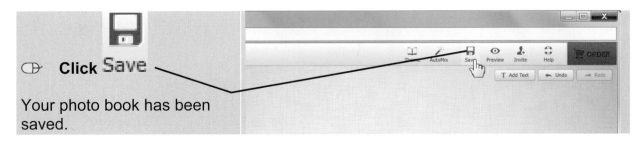

Your photo book has been saved.

3.16 Adding Text to a Text Box

In *Mixbook* you can add text to text boxes. Here is how to do that:

    Click the text box

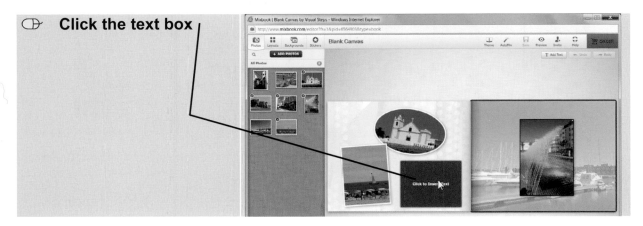

You can start typing at once. The text "click to insert text" will immediately be replaced by your own text.

Type: `Title of this fragment`

Press `Enter ←`

Type some text, for example, what you see here in this image

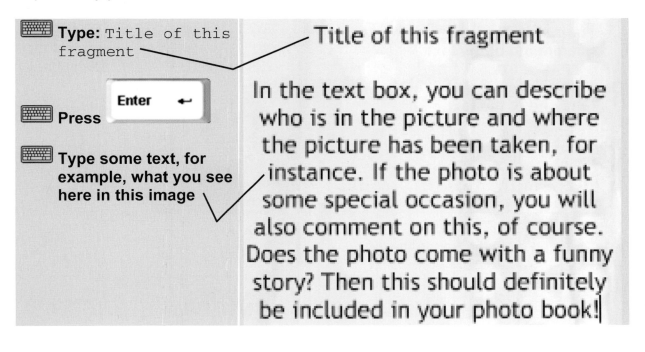

Title of this fragment

In the text box, you can describe who is in the picture and where the picture has been taken, for instance. If the photo is about some special occasion, you will also comment on this, of course. Does the photo come with a funny story? Then this should definitely be included in your photo book!

⊕ **Click next to the text box** —

The text has been added:

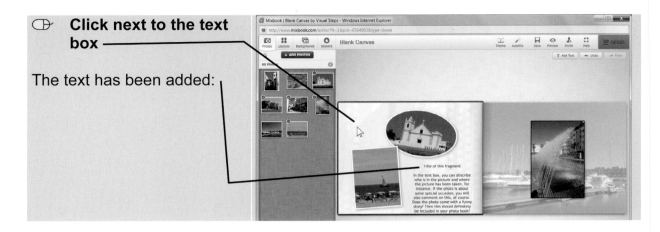

3.17 Formatting Text

As you can see, the title and the text are centered by default. In this case, it will look better if you align the text to the left:

⊕ **Position the mouse pointer at the beginning of the text**

⊕ **Drag downwards to the end of the text**

Now the text has been selected.

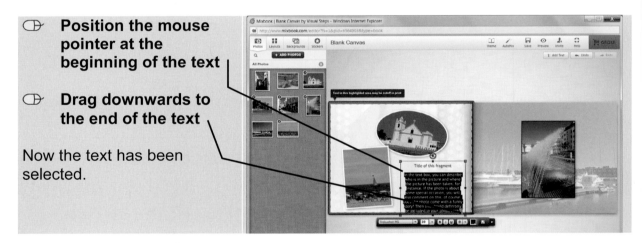

Now you can align the text to the left:

⊕ **By** ≣ **, click** ▾

⊕ **Click** ≣ Left

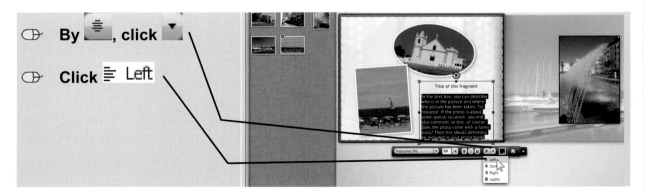

In the text box, you can edit the text in the same way as in *WordPad* or *Word*. For example, you can make the title appear in larger letters and make it bold. First, you need to select the title:

☞ **Click the title three times**

Now the title has been selected.

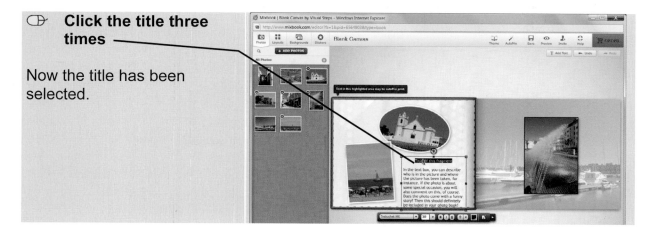

Now you can change the font size:

☞ **By** 20 **, click** ▼

☞ **Drag the scroll bar upwards until you reach** 24

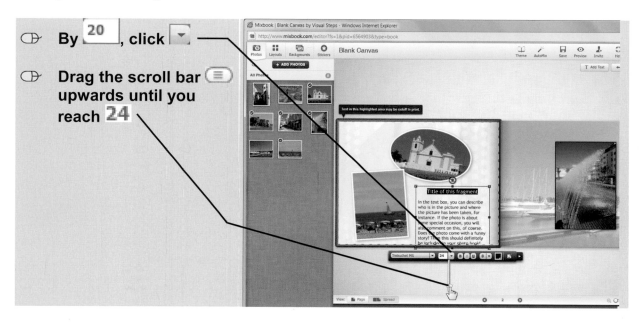

Now the title appears in larger letters. You can also make the title bold and italic:

Click **B**

Click **I**

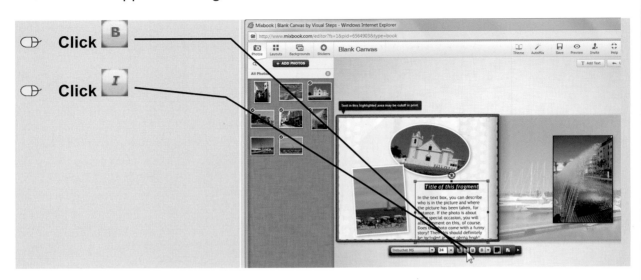

You can even change the color of the title text:

Click

Click (blue)

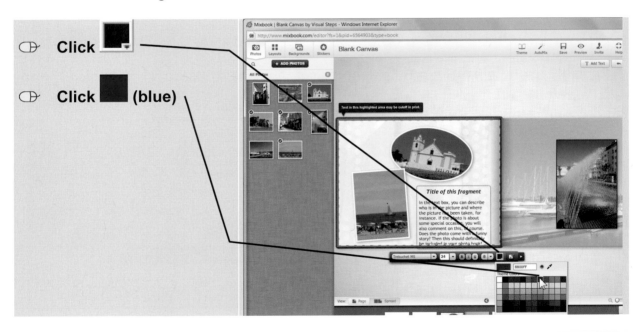

Click next to the text box

Now you will see that the title is displayed in bold and italic letters:

But the text is still running across the photos. You learned previously in this chapter how to reduce and move a text box.

☞ **Try to reduce the text box or move it in such a way, that there is no longer any text appearing on top of the photo** 🐾⁵

3.18 Adding a Text Box

If there are too few text boxes on a page, you can always add an extra text box yourself. Just try it:

☞ **Click the right page**

☞ **Click** T Add Text

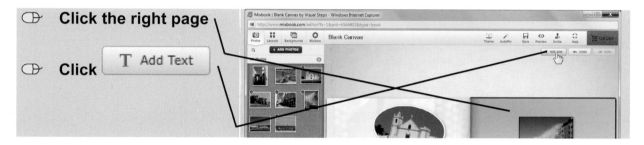

The new text box will placed on the photo. You are going to drag it to a position next to the photo:

☞ **Click the text box**

☞ **Drag the text box to the top left**

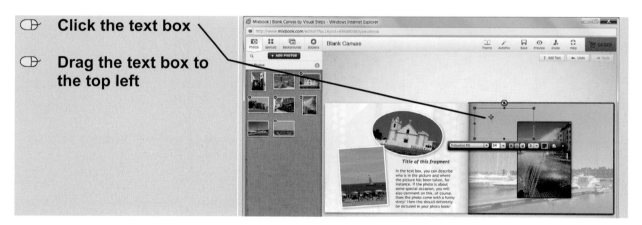

Now you are going to enlarge the text box:

☞ **Click the text box**

☞ **Put the mouse pointer on the handle it the middle of the right-hand side**

☞ **Drag the handle to the left**

☞ **Put the mouse pointer on the handle it the middle of the bottom side**

☞ **Drag the handle downwards**

Now the text box has been enlarged.

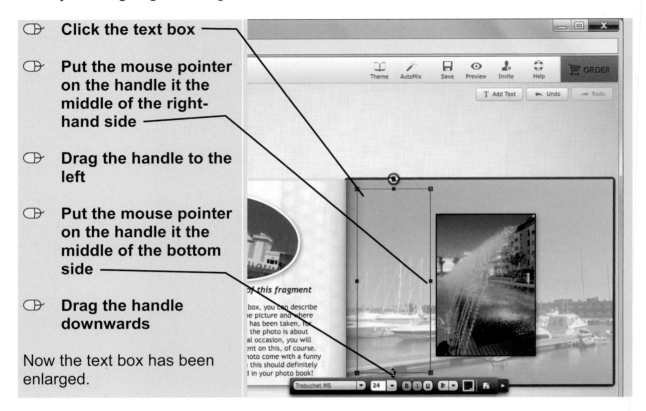

3.19 Copying Text from a Text Editing Program

You can add as many text boxes to the photo book as you want. It is up to you to decide how much text there is going to be and how many text boxes you will need to spread out the text.
If you want to write a longer text, and maybe do a little editing before inserting it into the photo book, it is useful to use a text editing program. At a later stage, you can copy the text from the text editor to the text boxes in the photo book.

☞ **Open *WordPad*** 🐾[6]

☞ **Change the font size to 12 points** 🐾[7]

Type: Copying text

Press Enter ↵

Type the text from the image you see here

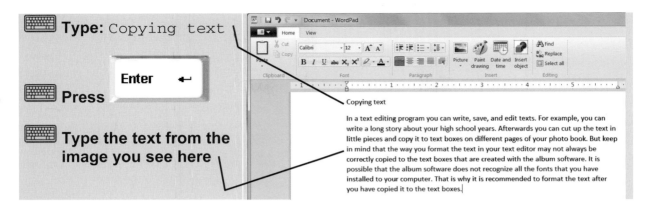

You can copy this longer text to a text box in the photo book. Here is how to do that:

Position the mouse pointer at the beginning of the text

Drag downwards to the end of the text

Now the text has been selected.

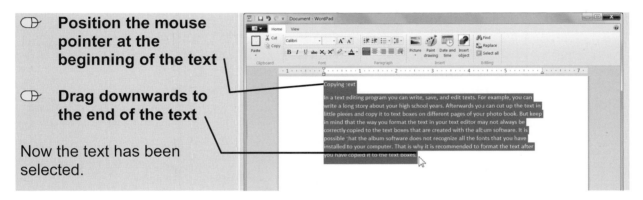

Now you are going to copy the text:

Click Copy

In *Windows Vista* and *XP*:

Click Edit

Click Copy

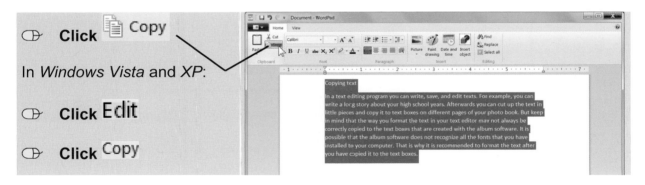

The text has been copied to your *Clipboard*. Now go back to *Mixbook*:

☞ **Open the *Mixbook* window from the taskbar** ✂️8

Once again, you will see the *Mixbook* window:

☞ **Right-click the text box**

☞ **Click Paste**

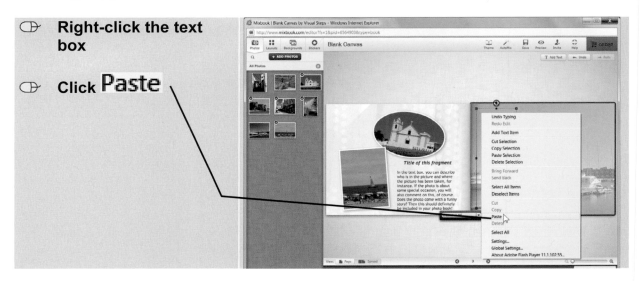

The copied text has been added:

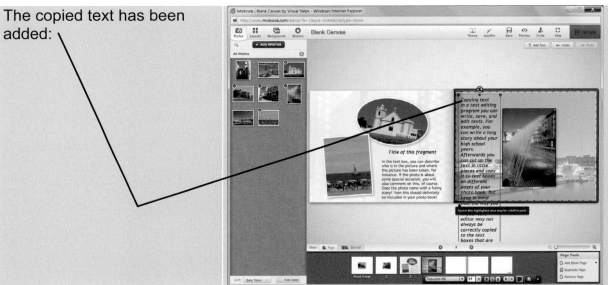

The size of the text box adjusts automatically, so that it fits the entire text. The text will be formatted according to the last formatting you made in a text box. You can change that now:

☞ **Change the text color to black** 🐾⁹

☞ **Make sure that the text is not italic and bold** 🐾¹⁰

☞ **Change the font size to 16** 🐾⁷

☞ **Click next to the text box**

Now the text is displayed next to the photo:

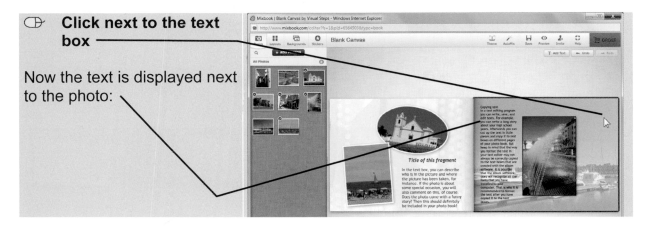

While you are creating your photo album, you can always zoom in to view the details up close. Here is how to do that:

In the bottom right-hand corner of the window, you will see a slider:

☞ **Drag the slider ○ a bit to the right**

The double page will be displayed in a larger size. To view the right-hand page:

☞ **Drag the frame**

to the right page

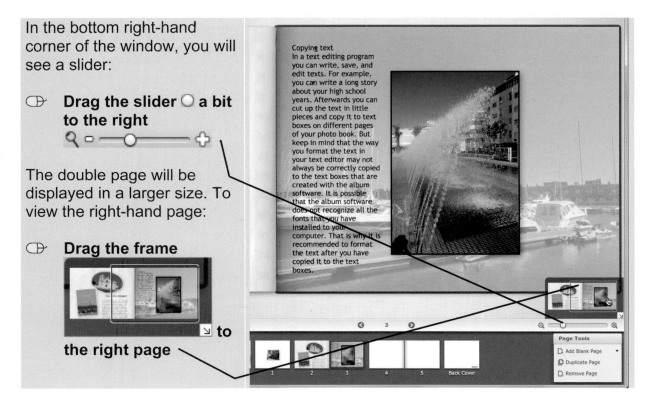

Now you can zoom out again, in order to view both pages of the photo book:

In the bottom right-hand corner of the window:

☞ **Drag the slider ⬭ completely to the left**

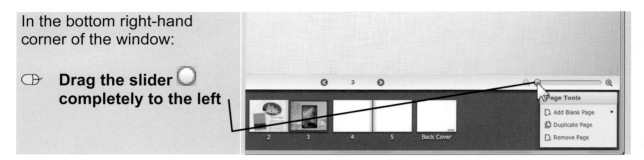

Now you can close *WordPad*:

☞ **Close *WordPad* and do not save the text** ✂️³

💡 **Tip**

View examples in a larger size
On the website that accompanies this book, you can view examples of the album pages shown in this book in a larger size. Here is how to do that:

☞ **Open *Internet Explorer*** ✂️¹

☞ **Go to the www.visualsteps.com/photobook webpage**

☞ Click **Examples**

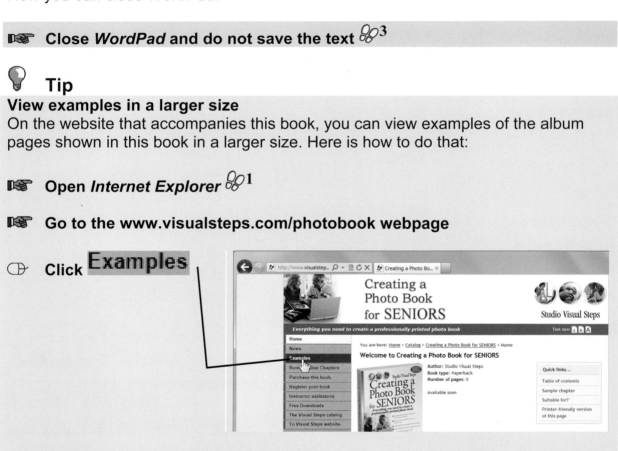

You see the examples of the album pages.

In the following section you will learn how to add and delete pages.

3.20 Adding and Deleting Pages

In this chapter you have edited pages in the photo book, as an exercise. When you start creating your own photo book, you will probably want to add more pages. By *Mixbook,* the minimum number of pages is 20. The current maximum number of pages is 99, but the *Mixbook* website says they are working on increasing the page limit.

This is how you add two more pages:

Click Add Blank Page

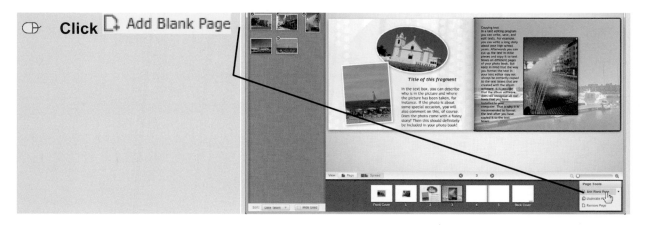

The two new pages will be added after the page you were currently working on:

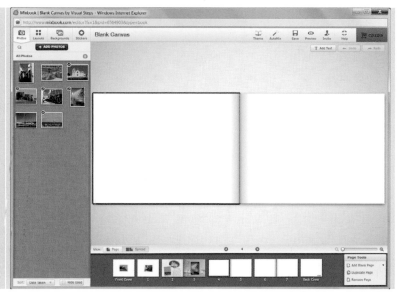

Tip

Pages with the same layout
If you want to add pages that have the same layout as the previous pages, then just do this:

⊕ **Click** 🗐 Duplicate Page

If you have added too many pages, you can delete these pages one at a time. This is how to delete the pages you are currently viewing:

⊕ **Click** 🗋 Remove Page

⊕ **Click** 🗋 Remove Page
  once more

Now the pages have been deleted:

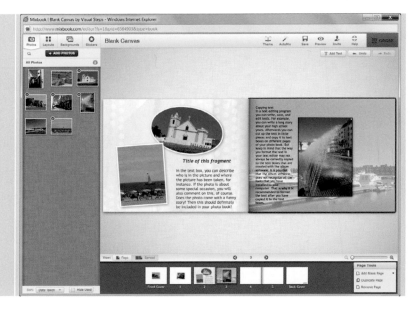

3.21 Changing the Order of the Pages

Perhaps you're not completely satisfied with the order of the pages. You can easily change the order of the pages.

☞ **If necessary, flip through the pages to page 2 and 3** ⸾⸾^{11}

☞ **Add two new pages** ⸾⸾^{12}

This is how you can move page 2 and 3 to page 4 and 5:

⊕ **Position the mouse pointer under**

on

Move Spread

⊕ **Drag the pages to**

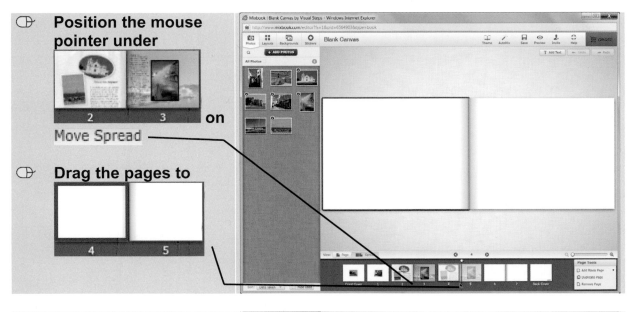

Now page 2 and 3 are blank. The two edited pages have moved over to page 4 and 5:

You can also move the pages back again, one at a time:

⊕ **Position the mouse**

pointer on

⊕ **Drag the page to**

☞ **Move page 5 back to page 3** 🦶13

You can also switch two single pages around. Just try this with pages 2 and 3:

⊕ **Position the mouse**

pointer on

⊕ **Drag the page to**

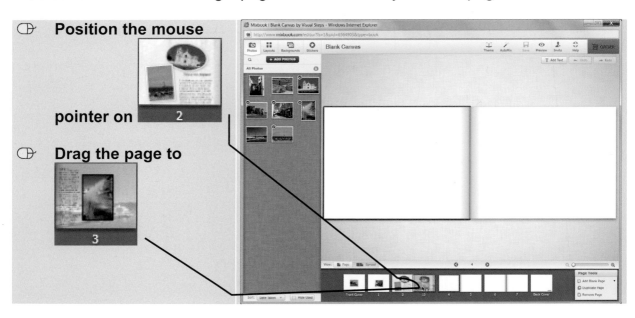

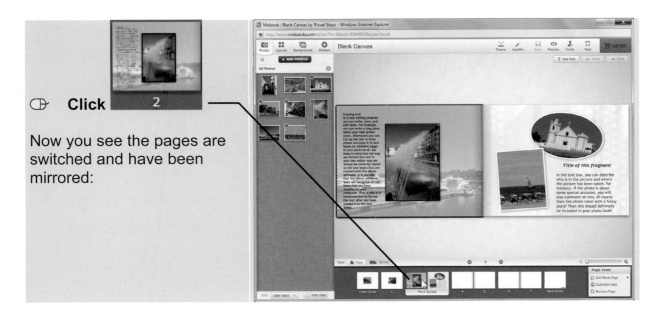

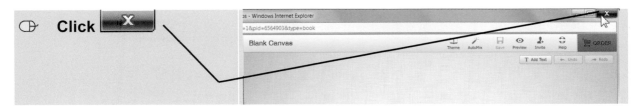

⊕ **Click** [2]

Now you see the pages are switched and have been mirrored:

3.22 Closing Mixbook

Most likely, you will not be able to finish your photo book with all its photos and text in a single day. You can close the program and continue working at a later date.

⊕ **Click** [X]

You work will automatically be saved and you logged out.

☞ **Close** *Internet Explorer* 🐾³

3.23 Viewing a Preview

After you have completed a number of pages of your photo book, you can take a look at a preview of your book. This is how you open the *preview*:

☞ **Open** *Internet Explorer* 🐾¹

☞ **Go to the www.mixbook.com webpage** 🐾²

Click Login

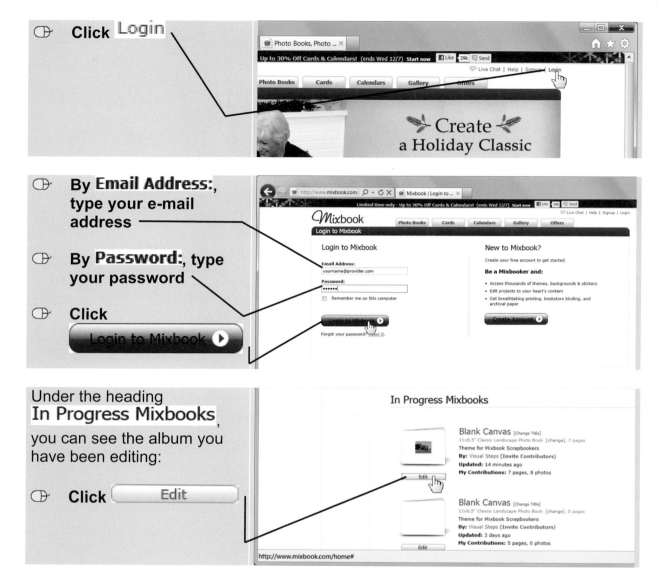

By **Email Address:**, type your e-mail address

By **Password:**, type your password

Click

By **Login to Mixbook**

Under the heading **In Progress Mixbooks**, you can see the album you have been editing:

Click **Edit**

Mixbook will be opened. You see the *Welcome to Mixbook!* window:

Click ⊗

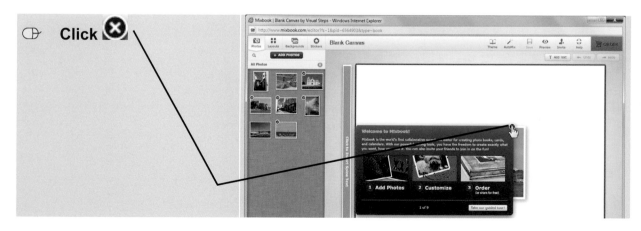

To see a preview of the album:

In the right-hand side of the window:

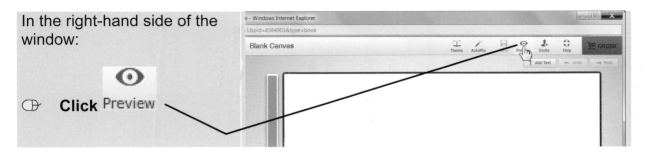

⊕ **Click** Preview

Now the photo book will be opened. This is to browse through the book:

⊕ **Click Next** ⏵⏵

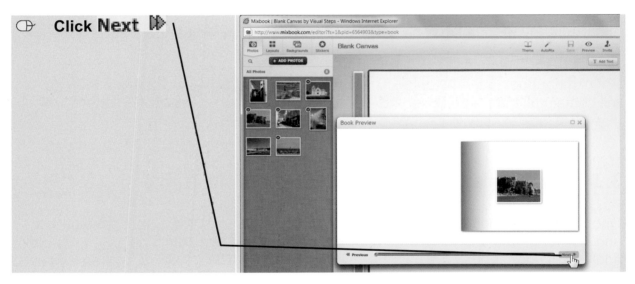

You will see the next page:

If you want to close the preview:

⊕ **Click** ✕

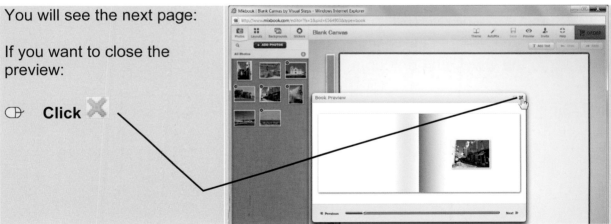

If you are not satisfied, you can edit the album further.

☞ Close *Mixbook* ✌³

☞ Close *Internet Explorer* ✌³

↳ **Please note!**

The text in the preview window might not be clearly visible. But when the photo album is printed, the text will be both readable and sharp.

💡 **Tip**

Check carefully

Use the preview window, above all, when you have nearly finished your photo album and it is ready for printing. The preview will give you a clear picture of what the book will look like once it is printed.

Check your book page by page. This way, you will be certain that the printed version will contain all the photo boxes, text boxes and backgrounds you have added and that it will look exactly like what you had in mind.

3.24 Sending and Paying for Your Photo Book

Once you have finished your photo book, you can send it to the album print service and pay for it. In a short time, the book will be sent to your home address or another address of your choosing. To do this, you need to open the *Mixbook* program again.

☞ Open *Internet Explorer* ✌¹

☞ Go to the www.mixbook.com webpage ✌²

☞ Sign in at *Mixbook* ✌¹⁴

The album you have been editing, will be displayed under **In Progress Mixbooks**.

To send the album to the print service:

☞ **Click** Order

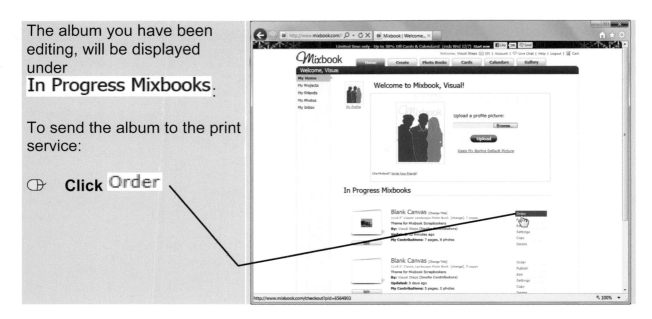

In the next window you will see an overview of all the elements that make up your order, and the price of the order. If you agree, you can finalize your order:

Here you can enter the number of copies you want to order: ─────

Now you need to enter an address for the recipient:

☞ **Click** add

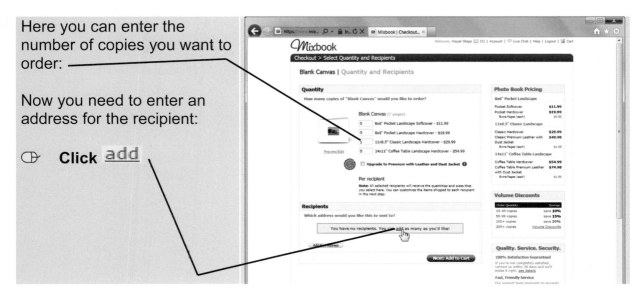

💡 **Tip**

Search the Internet for a discount code

Mixbook regularly offers discounts in their newsletter. It is also worth your while to search the Internet for current discount codes or coupons. This may save you 10 to 20% of the printing costs of your book. They sometimes even offer a free (second) copy of the book.

If you type the keywords *Mixbook discount* in the *Google* search box, you will get many results. Make sure that the discount codes you find are still current. If not, search for a current code.

☞ **Enter your personal data**

⊕ **Click** **Save**

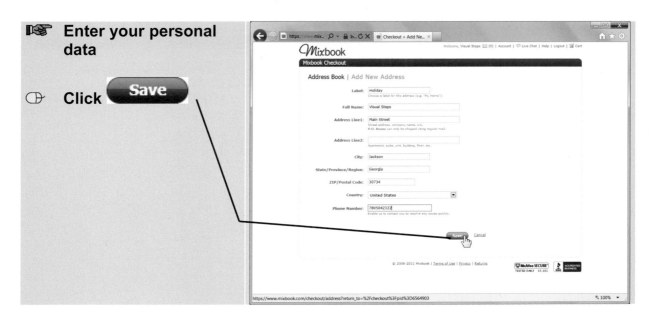

Now you have entered the address. You can continue with the ordering procedure:

⊕ **Check the box ☑ next to the address**

⊕ **Click** **Next: Add to Cart**

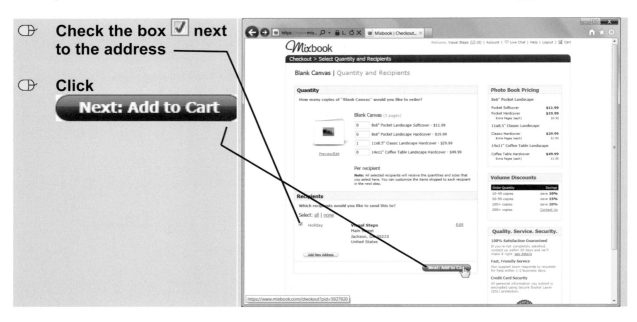

Since this album only contains five pages, you will see a message indicating that the photo book needs to contain at least twenty pages. When you are creating your own album, you need to make sure that the album contains sufficient pages.

☞ Check your order

If you have found a discount code, you can type the code, and then click **Apply** :

⊕ **Click** Checkout >>

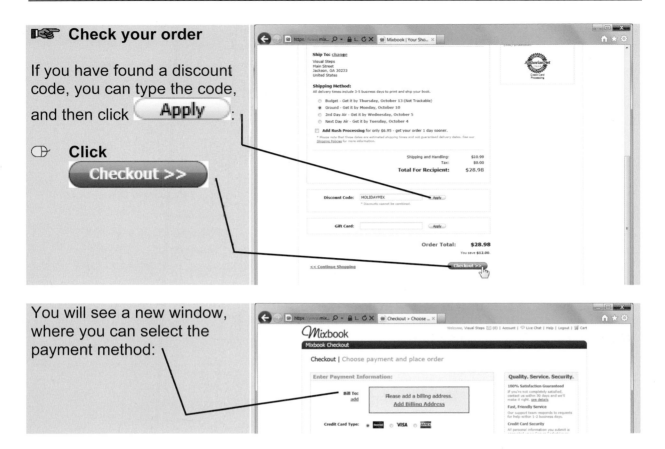

You will see a new window, where you can select the payment method:

Mixbook accepts payment by VISA, MasterCard, and American Express credit cards. A secure SSL connection will lead you to a window where you can enter your credit card information and other personal data.

☞ Follow the instructions in the windows

After you have concluded the payment procedure, you can log out:

⊕ **Click** Logout

☞ Close *Internet Explorer* ⏿³

Now you have acquired the necessary skills to create a book in which you can tell your story, using photos and text. In *Chapter 4 Writing Tips* and *Chapter 5 Formatting Tips* you will find a number of useful tips to help you further. In the following chapters and the bonus chapter *Working with Picaboo* on **www.visualsteps.com/photobook** you can find inspiration for creating books on all kinds of different subjects.

3.25 Background Information

Dictionary

Adobe Reader	Free program that enables you to open and print PDF files.
Frame	Stylized borders that you can use to frame a picture.
Pixel	The smallest element that is used to compose a digital image, also called a dot.
Resolution	The photo definition, determined by the number of pixels in the photo.
Shape (Mask)	Creative cutout of a photo, in a specific shape.

3.26 Tips

 Tip

Editing photos
Mixbook offers a number of options you can use to edit and enhance your photos.

   Click the photo you want to edit

Now you will see a toolbar below the photo. Here is an overview of all the functions in the toolbar:

: set the brightness, contrast, color depth and shade.

: rotate the photo to the right.

: flip horizontally.

: list of styles applicable to an image.

: list of effects applicable to an image.

Please note: editing a photo will not affect the original photo. You will only modify the way in which the photo is displayed in the album.

Tip

Publish your photo book
After you have signed in to *Mixbook*, you can publish your photo album online:

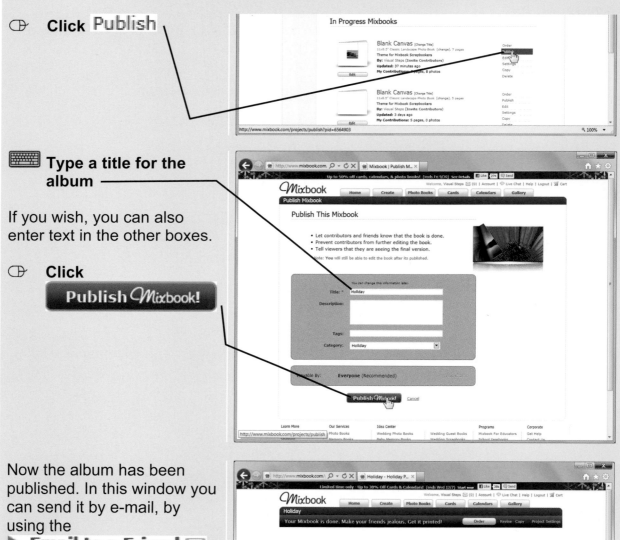

⬡ **Click** Publish

⌨ **Type a title for the album**

If you wish, you can also enter text in the other boxes.

⬡ **Click** Publish *Mixbook!*

Now the album has been published. In this window you can send it by e-mail, by using the

▶ **Email to a Friend**

button, or share the album on *Facebook* by clicking

Like :

Tip

Theme for a photo book
Mixbook contains a number of themes you can use while creating your photo book. Perhaps you would like to use a seasonal theme, such as summer or winter or a travel theme. There are also many predefined themes for special occasions such as weddings, a new baby and holidays.

☞ **Click the desired theme**

☞ **Click**

Choose Theme >

Now the photo album will be created. You can insert your photos into the photo boxes:

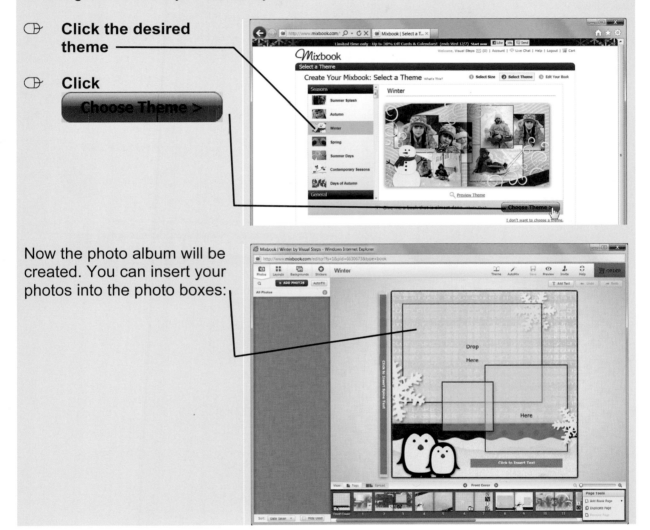

Tip

Adding stickers

While you are editing your photo album, you can add stickers to embellish your pages, and make them even more appealing. Here is to do that:

In the left-hand side of the window:

⊕ **Click**

You will see an overview of various stickers:

⊕ **Drag the desired sticker(s) to the photo album**

4. Writing Tips

For many people, writing a text or a letter does not come easy. Some of us can effortlessly write pages and pages, while others need a couple of hours just to write a few lines down. There may be various causes for this. Maybe you just do not have enough inspiration to start writing your story. Or maybe you are insecure about your style of writing. In this case, you may find it helpful to read some of the tips this book offers.

The writing tips in this book will help you get started and will make writing your story easier. You will also learn how to avoid some well-known 'writers' pitfalls'. As a result, your story will become more attractive and pleasant to read.

Still looking for inspiration? You may be able to pick up a good idea or two with some of the inspiring photo book examples we have provided. You can use these ideas and build upon them for your own project. In the last chapters of this book you will find examples covering a wide range of topics.

In this chapter you will learn how to improve your writing, on the basis of the following ten writing tips:

- answer the familiar questions;
- use the inspiration chapters in this book;
- write as if you were telling a story;
- keep in mind for whom you are writing;
- choose the correct form;
- use the correct tense;
- do not make your sentences too long;
- write actively;
- do not repeat yourself;
- do not be afraid of blank spaces.

4.1 Ten Writing Tips

The ten writing tips in this chapter will not only help you how to write more fluently, they will also help you to write a pleasant and easy-to-read story.

1. Answer the Familiar Questions

A photo book is about telling a story using photos with text. Use the photos you have selected as a source of inspiration for writing the accompanying text. The easiest way to start is by answering a few familiar questions concerning the photo:

- **who** is in the picture?
- **who** has taken the picture?
- **where** has the photo been taken?
- **when** has the photo been taken?
- **why** has the photo been taken?
- **what** else do you see on the photo?

First, answer the questions short and to the point. These could be some answers to these questions, for instance:

- **who** is in the picture?   *my cousin Yvonne from Canada and me*
- **who** took the picture?   *my husband Michael*
- **where** was the photo taken?   *at a restaurant on the beach in Mendocino*
- **when** was the photo taken?   *at the beginning of April 2011*
- **why w**as the photo taken?   *as a reminder of a great day*
- **what** else do you see in the photo? *sun, sun glasses, clouds, wind, terrace*

The answers to these questions should give you something to start with. Just by describing this photo you will have a small amount of text. In the next step, you can turn the short answers into longer sentences.

Like this, for example:

In this picture you see me and my cousin Yvonne from Canada. Michael took this picture when we were sitting on a terrace at Mendocino beach, in the beginning of April 2011. The photo is a nice reminder of a pleasant, sunny day. It was very windy. Only a few people wanted to sit out on the terrace, but we welcomed the sunshine!

You see, it has already become a little story. But the sentences are not yet flowing, and the story does not tell us a whole lot yet. Try to re-write the story once again and complement it with other memories you can think of.

 Tip

Order
When re-writing the story you can always change the order of the sentences.

This might be the result if you add some of your other recollections:

My cousin Yvonne came over from Canada in April 2011, to visit her family and friends. At a certain point we discovered she had never been to a Californian beach. Well, that could be easily taken care of! On a Sunday, Michael, Yvonne and I went to Mendocino. We traveled along the coast: watching the dolphins, walking along the beach, visiting the Kelley House Museum. We had a delicious lunch at a beach restaurant. There was a lot of wind, but we were sheltered by a glass wall and the sun was warm enough. Not many people realized this, because the terrace was nearly empty. We did not notice Michael taking this picture; otherwise we would have put on a happy face!

2. Use the Inspiration Chapters in This Book

The inspiration chapters in this book can help you to compose your own story. Here you will find examples and ideas for album stories on a wide range of topics: a travel story, a life history, an account of a wedding day, etcetera.

The inspiration chapters are written by using examples of titles and headings as a basis. Each sample title comes with a number of questions which will help you write your story.

Use the same working method as with the previous tip:
* answer the questions short and to the point;
* convert the short answers into longer sentences;
* re-write the story and add any other memories or anecdotes you can think of.

 Tip

Inspiration chapters
In this book you will find the following inspiration chapters:
Chapter 7 Create a Vacation Photo Book
Chapter 8 Create a Wedding Day Book
Chapter 9 Tell Your Life Story
Chapter 10 Write About a Baby's First Year

3. Write As If You Were Telling a Story

Often, people will suddenly start using more formal language when they have to write a story. As if everything needs to be much neater and tidier once it is written down. Usually, this results in complicated, artificial sentences. It is better to adopt a style where you write things down as if you were telling someone about your ideas.

Do not linger too long if you are not sure about the correct spelling or grammar in a sentence. Just as you would not bother with this if you were telling a story. Write the word or sentence the way you think it should be and just keep on writing. In the first writing, the content is much more important than the style.

If you run out of inspiration for new lines, then re-read what you have written earlier. You might decide to delete some parts that strike you as superfluous. Or maybe you want to change the order of the sentences.

 Tip

Read aloud (1)
The easiest way of finding out if a text is fluent is to read the text out loud. You will immediately notice the sentences that are not quite so fluent.

Once you are satisfied with the contents of your story, you can start checking the spelling and grammar.

Tip

Spelling and grammar

Are spelling and grammar your weaker points? Get a family member or friend who is good at this job to read your story. You can also decide to write your story by using a text editor, such as *Word*. This way, you can use the automatic spelling and grammar checker. Remain critical and take a careful look at the suggestions the program presents; do not blindly take over all the changes the text editor suggests.

4. Keep in Mind for Whom You Are Writing

For whom are you creating this photo book? For your children or grandchildren? For people of your own generation? If you are writing for a young child or grandchild, for instance, it is a good idea to cast a critical eye on your story:

- is the text too tedious for young people?
- will they be interested in your story?
- does the text contain words or terms that are unknown to them?

The terminology from the days that you were enlisted may be very unfamiliar to your grandchildren, while your old buddies will know exactly what you are talking about. Keep in mind for whom you are writing and add some extra information for them, explain things where space is available.

5. Choose the Correct Form

If you are creating a story about your own life, it is best to use the first person singular (I …). Writing in the third person singular (he/she …) will create a distance between you and your audience. It is easier to write about your ideas and feelings if you use the first person.

Just take a look at the difference between:

On the third day she visited Paris. The Eiffel tower was the highlight of the day. Standing on the highest platform you have a beautiful view.

and

On the third day I visited Paris. I was especially impressed by our visit to the Eiffel tower. I could not get enough of the view from the highest platform.

6. Use the Correct Tense

Make sure you keep using the same tense throughout the whole story. If you start telling a story by using the past tense (once upon a time), you should not suddenly switch to the present tense (nowadays). In this example we have mixed up the past and present tenses:

Hank and Patty were doing the dishes together. All of a sudden, somebody bangs the window. Patty is startled and dropped a cup.

This is what the sentence would look like in the present tense:

Hank and Patty are doing the dishes together. All of a sudden, somebody bangs the window. Patty is startled and drops a cup.

And this is the same sentence, but now in the past tense:

Hank and Patty were doing the dishes together. All of a sudden, somebody banged the window. Patty was startled and dropped a cup.

Of course, it is up to you whether you want to use the past or present tense. But once you have decided, do not change the tense later on, especially within the same sentence.

7. Do not Use Very Long Sentences

If you use long sentences, separated by various commas, your readers will lose track of your story. They will need to re-read the sentence in order to understand what you want to say. It might annoy your readers so much that they do not want to continue reading and decide to leave the story for what it is. That is why you need to keep your sentences short and simple.

For example:

Since Milly, our neighbor's cat, was suddenly spotted in the park, almost two years after she ran away from home, last week, her owners, who had given up all hope of ever seeing her again, have posted her photo in all kinds of places, and searched the park every evening, until they finally found her.

If you split up this extremely long sentence in a few shorter parts, it can be like this:

Almost two years after she ran away from home, Milly was finally spotted in the park. Our neighbors had given up all hope of ever seeing their cat again. Last week, they posted her photo again in many different places. After having searched the park for several evenings, they finally found her.

In this way, the text is much easier to read, more lively, even exciting.

 Tip

Read aloud (2)
Read your text out loud, once more. Do you need to stop for air in mid-sentence?
Then the sentence is too long. It is better to split it into two separate sentences.

 Please note!
On the other hand, do not make the sentences too short. This might come across as
a bit childish.

8. Write Actively

Do you still know the difference between the *active* and *passive construction*?

This is an example of a passive construction:

The dishes were done by Hank and Patty.

In an active form, the sentence looks like this:

Hank and Patty did the dishes.

If you use the active construction, your texts will be easier and more pleasant to read.

9. Do Not Repeat Yourself

Try to avoid using the same word twice in a short space. For instance:

From our window we could see a big building. This building appeared to be empty.

It is better to look for a synonym for the word 'building'. You could use the word
'premises', for example. Then the sentence would look like this:

From our window we could see a big building. The premises appeared to be empty.

 Tip

Dictionary of Synonyms
Are you having a hard time trying to think of a specific synonym? In that case, use a
dictionary of synonyms. There are several websites that offer lists of synonyms.

10. Do Not Be Afraid of Blank Spaces

Many readers find it difficult to read large amounts of uninterrupted text. A page containing lots of text will look much more attractive and be easier to read if you insert a blank line now and again.

Just take a look at the difference:

Program:
Blurb Booksmart

Text without blank lines

Program:
Blurb Booksmart

Text with blank lines

The page with the blank lines is much more inviting to the reader. The page without the blank lines will rather deter the reader.

In this chapter you have been presented with ten writing tips, which will help you write much better stories more easily. In the next chapter you will find a number of tips for formatting your album pages.

5. Formatting Tips

Not only does photo book software enable you to add photos and text quickly and easily to a photo book, there are usually a whole slew of options available for formatting the pages.

By choosing the right layout and page format, you can influence the appearance, the character and tone of the album. In this chapter you will find many examples of page formatting. We will give you tips on how to ensure that your story is as pleasant and as easy to read as possible.

It's possible to select a different design for each and every page. But a consistent format and uniformity in design will make your album look more coherent. This chapter will also give you tips to achieve cohesiveness in the design.

In this chapter you will learn how to:

- influence the character and tone of the album by choosing the right formatting options;
- enhance the readability of the text;
- check the album design for certain specific items.

 Please note!

Below each album page example in this chapter we will list the album software and the formatting options that were used. Be aware that most providers of album software are steadily honing and improving their programs. It may occur that a certain background, template, frame, or font becomes unavailable.

5.1 Character of the Page

By formatting the page in a certain way you can influence the character, tone or mood of the page. In this section you will find a number of formatting examples, where the same page will look very different by using alternative designs.

Calm

If you use a neutral background, the page will look quiet and calm. This way, the photos on the page will get full attention. By straightening the photos and aligning them with the text, the page will become even more pleasant and easy to read.

Our granddaughter Sophia

Here are two photos of our granddaughter Sophia. Once she realized how much attention she got with her big smile, there was no stopping her. As soon as somebody pointed a camera at her, she seemed to turn into a fashion model and flashed her enormous smile! In this picture she is about five months old.

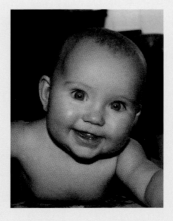

But where food is concerned, Sophia makes an exception: that is serious business, no smiles there! The photo of her holding her first ice cream has been taken when she was nine months old. Her older sister Karin got an ice cream and Sophia did not agree: she wanted one too!

Program:
Blurb BookSmart

Standard background color

Font:
Bodoni MT Black (title)
Arial (text)

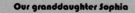

Our granddaughter Sophia

Here are two photos of our granddaughter Sophia. Once she realized how much attention she got with her big smile, there was no stopping her. As soon as somebody pointed a camera at her, she seemed to turn into a fashion model and flashed her enormous smile! In this picture she is about five months old.

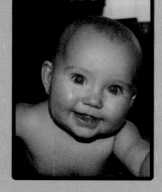

But where food is concerned, Sophia makes an exception: that is serious business, no smiles there! The photo of her holding her first ice cream has been taken when she was nine months old. Her older sister Karin got an ice cream and Sophia did not agree: she wanted one too!

Program:
Blurb BookSmart

Standard background color

Border applied to the photos

Font:
Bauhaus 93 (title)
Times New Roman (text)

Calm and Romantic

A background with soft colors and reflections will create a romantic effect for your album page:

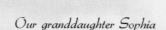

Our granddaughter Sophia

Here are two photos of our granddaughter Sophia. Once she realized how much attention she got with her big smile, there was no stopping her. As soon as somebody pointed a camera at her, she seemed to turn into a fashion model and flashed her enormous smile! In this picture she is about five months old.

But where food is concerned, Sophia makes an exception: that is serious business, no smiles there! The photo of her holding her first ice cream has been taken when she was nine months old. Her older sister Karin got an ice cream and Sophia did not agree: she wanted one too!

Program:
Mixbook

Standard background photo across two pages 76% transparency

Reflection Style applied to photos

Font:
Gabrielle

Calm and Nostalgic

Most album software will let you add special effects to the photos. For example, you can convert the photo to black-and-white. If you combine this with a white border around the photos, the page will look nostalgic and stylish.

Our granddaughter Sophia

Here are two photos of our granddaughter Sophia. Once she realized how much attention she got with her big smile, there was no stopping her. As soon as somebody pointed a camera at her, she seemed to turn into a fashion model and flashed her enormous smile! In this picture she is about five months old.

But where food is concerned, Sophia makes an exception: that is serious business, no smiles there! The photo of her holding her first ice cream has been taken when she was nine months old. Her older sister Karin got an ice cream and Sophia did not agree: she wanted one too!

Program:
Mixbook

Standard background color

Border applied to the photos

Font:
Sort Mill Goudy

Humorous, Surprising

You can create a nice effect by using a light-colored text on a darker background. A white or yellow text set against a dark background will still be easy to read. By adding frames to the pictures, the page will have quite a different impact.

Our granddaughter Sophia

Here are two photos of our granddaughter Sophia. Once she realized how much attention she got with her big smile, there was no stopping her. As soon as somebody pointed a camera at her, she seemed to turn into a fashion model and flashed her enormous smile! In this picture she is about five months old.

But where food is concerned, Sophia makes an exception: that is serious business, no smiles there! The photo of her holding her first ice cream has been taken when she was nine months old. Her older sister Karin got an ice cream and Sophia did not agree: she wanted one too!

Program:
Mixbook

Standard background color

Stickers added from theme Born To Be Wild

Font:
Lane Narrow (title)
Comic Sans MS (text)

Vibrant Background

A background with strong colors and a pattern will make the page seem more vibrant. The reader will pay less attention to the photos and the text. This effect will be enhanced by adding a rim around the photos (framing). Take caution when using busy backgrounds. They will make the text less easy to read.

Program:
Mixbook

Standard background

Border with sticker
applied to the photos

Font:
Cooper Black (title)
Arial (text)

Flashy

By using bright colors your page will look flashy and modern. But some people may complain that it hurts their eyes. You can enhance the trendy appearance even more by rotating the photo boxes and adding a background color to the text boxes. By choosing the same color for the text box and the frame, you will immediately be able to see which text goes with which photo.

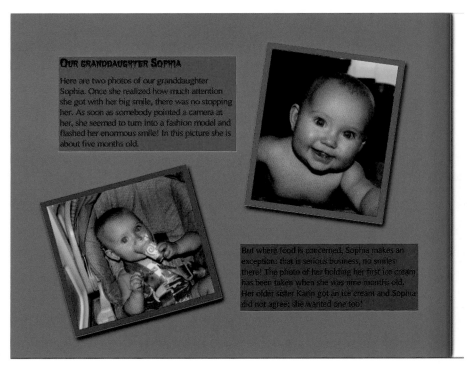

Program:
Picaboo

Standard background color

Self-defined borders

Font:
Dracula (title)
RomanSerif (text)

Stickers

If you add stickers to the page, the page will look more playful, but also more crowded. In the example below the clip art illustrations look very cheerful, but the multitude of pictures is distracting and the focus is no longer on the content of the page.

Program: Mixbook

Standard background photo across two pages

Stickers added

Font: Bentham

You can also do it this way, with less stickers:

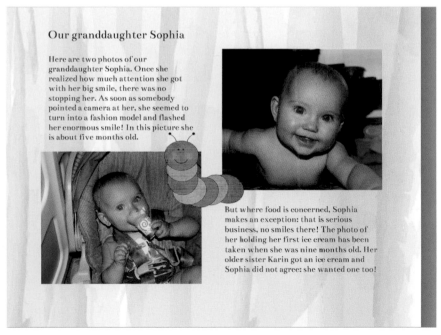

Program: Mixbook

Standard background photo across two pages

Sticker added

Font: Bentham

Tip

Stickers only available in Mixbook
A large collection of stickers is only available within the *Mixbook* and *Shutterfly* photo book software. *Blurb* and *Picaboo* also offer small pictures, but you can only add these as ornaments at the top of a page or near the corner of a photo.

 Tip

The best is the enemy of the good
Of course it is nice to have some variation and add some lively pages now and again. But try to avoid adding lots of formatting effects to each and every page of your photo book. Your readers will soon get tired of pages full of crowded backgrounds, wild fonts, frames and lots of clip art.

 Tip

View examples in larger size
On the website that accompanies this book, you can view examples of the album pages shown in this book in a larger size. Go to **www.visualsteps.com/photobook**

5.2 Readability of the Text

When you create a photo book, the text is just as important as the photos and illustrations. That is why you need to make sure your text is easily readable, and you should take this into account while you are formatting the pages.

Background

In this example you can see how the obtrusive background with the Gummi Bears diminishes the readability of the text:

Program:
Shutterfly

Photo as background

Font:
Bookman

If you display the same text against the softer, faded background photo of a teddy bear, the text is much easier to read:

Our granddaughter Sophia

Here are two photos of our granddaughter Sophia. Once she realized how much attention she got with her big smile, there was no stopping her. As soon as somebody pointed a camera at her, she seemed to turn into a fashion model and flashed her enormous smile! In this picture she is about five months old.

But where food is concerned, Sophia makes an exception: that is serious business, no smiles there! The photo of her holding her first ice cream has been taken when she was nine months old. Her older sister Karin got an ice cream and Sophia did not agree: she wanted one too!

*Program:
Shutterfly*

Photo as background

*Font:
Bookman*

 Tip

Blur the background
Nearly all photo book software programs contain an option for blurring, or fading the background photos. You can also do this with your own background photo. Here is how to do that in *Mixbook*:

☞ **Add an image as a background**

☞ **Click** `More`

☞ **Drag the slider** ○ **by** `Color Opacity:`

Unfortunately, the *Blurb* software program does not allow you to blur or fade their standard background images or your own background photo.

 Tip

Busy background
If your background is too busy, this will affect the readability of the text. Use these busy backgrounds for pages that contain a small amount of text, and use a calm, faded or blurred background for pages with a lot of text.

Font

It may be very tempting to choose a beautiful, handwritten font for the stories in your album. But this will not have a positive effect on the readability of your text, as the example below illustrates:

Program:
Picaboo

Corner applied to the photos

Standard background photo

Font:
English

 Tip

Title
You can use a handwritten or script type font for a title or for the page headings. But for longer pieces of text it is better to select a font that is clear and easy to read.

Width of the Text Lines

If you are creating a photo book in the landscape shape, it is better not to make the text the same width as the page. In this format, the lines will become far too long for your readers.

You can see this in the example:

Program:
Picaboo

Standard background

Shape applied to the photos

Font:
Graffiti (title)
Arial (text)

It will be easier to read and the layout is more attractive if you render the text in two narrow columns:

Program:
Picaboo

Standard background

Shape applied to the photos

Font:
Graffiti (title)
Arial (text)

5.3 Formatting the Story Album as a Whole

In the previous sections you have read about the influence of the design on the character, mood or tone of the pages and the readability of the text. You can use the design of your pages to make sure the book comes across as a unified entity. Below you will find some tips for formatting the entire album:

Maintain the Tone

The design you choose for your pages needs to back up the contents of your story. For instance, a wedding day album will benefit from romantic, hazy backgrounds in soft tones, with black text. But an album about your child's or grandchild's first year will be more appealing to younger people if you use bright, rich colors and display the text in various contrasting colors.

You do not need to use the same background image all the time. But by using backgrounds that project the same sort of mood or tone you will introduce some uniformity to your photo book. If you were to choose a different tone for each individual page, the album may be too full of distraction and could give your readers an unstable impression.

Make Sure the Text Format is Consistent

You will also need to make some decisions regarding the formatting of the text in your photo book. By choosing an identical format for the longer portions of text, for the headers, and for the captions, you can create more uniformity in your album.

For example, keep this in mind:
- preferably select a single font, font size, and font color for all descriptive texts.
- select a single font, font size, and font color for the buttons.
- if the structure of your story requires it, you can make a distinction between titles/headers of chapters and titles/headers of paragraphs. Use a smaller font size for the paragraph titles and a larger one for the chapter titles.
- If you use captions for your photos, it is better to select a smaller font size for these captions. This will make it clear that a specific caption belongs to a specific photo. If possible, always insert the captions in the same position.

Once you have selected a certain format, stick to it and keep using it throughout the entire album. If you keep changing the design, it may create an unstable impression on your readers.

Use the Same Layout

The layout of a page is the ratio between the printed portion of a page (containing the text and photos) and the blank margins. You can improve the uniformity of your photo book by always using the same type of layout:

- always position the title/header at the same height on every page and use the same page margins.
- always use the same spacing between the headers and the text below. Usually, in books one or two 'blank lines' are used. You can select the relevant line spacing.
- use the same margins on the top and sides of the page for all your photos. If you are using the standard page layouts from the photo book software, this is done for you automatically.

 Tip

Go through it once again
While you are writing and compiling your photo book, you will be more occupied with telling the story and selecting the right photos than with formatting details. This is why it is a good idea to browse through the entire album once more, before sending it to the album printer. Do not pay attention to the contents, but just check the fonts you have used, the font sizes and font colors as well as the page layout.

In this chapter you have learned how to influence the character, readability and uniformity of your photo book by using specific formats and designs. In the following chapter you can read how to collect and organize the photos for your photo book.

6. Collecting Photos

There are different ways to collect the photos you need for your photo book. If you already have photos stored on your computer, you can copy or move them to a separate folder that will be used for your book.

If you have photos stored in your camera's memory, you can copy them to your computer. In this chapter you can read how to do this by using *Windows Explorer*.

Do you have a large collection of photo albums? Do you want to use some of the photos from these albums in your photo book? Then you can scan these photos and add them to the collection that will be used for your book. In this chapter we will explain how to do this in *Windows 7, Windows Vista* and *Windows XP*.

In this chapter you will learn how to:

- create a new folder;
- copy photos to the new folder;
- import photos from your digital camera;
- scan photos in *Windows 7* or *Windows Vista*;
- scan photos in *Windows XP*.

 Please note!

In order to do all of the exercises in this chapter, you will need to have a digital camera and a scanner. If you do not have one or both of these, just read through the sections in which these devices are used.

 Please note!

In the following examples, the process is explained for *Windows 7, Windows Vista* and also for *Windows XP*. *Windows 7* is our starting point; if the operations in *Windows Vista* or *Windows XP* are considerably different, we will add separate instructions for these programs.

6.1 Creating a New Folder

If you have lots of photos stored on your computer, it is a good idea to collect the photos you want to use for your photo book beforehand and copy them to a separate folder.

 Please note!

In this example we use the *Pictures* folder (*My Pictures* in *Windows XP*). You can make a new folder or subfolder in another location if you like, as long as you remember where you have placed it. This will not affect the following operations.

This is how to open the *Pictures* folder:

In *Windows 7* and *Vista*:

⊕ Click 🔵

⊕ Click **Pictures**

In *Windows XP*:

⊕ Click **start**

⊕ Click 📁 **My Pictures**

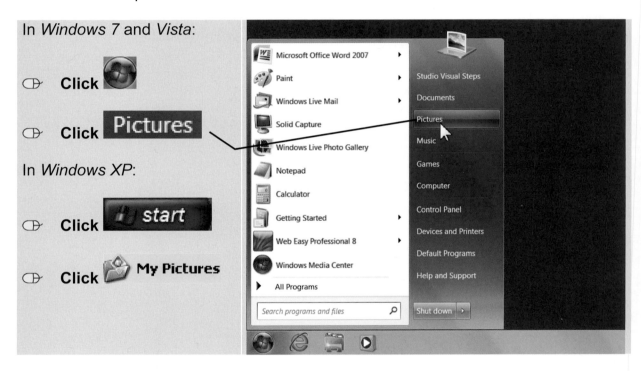

The *Pictures* folder (*My Pictures* in *Windows XP*, also called *Pictures* here, for the sake of convenience) will be opened:

In this example, the *Pictures* folder contains two subfolders:

The *Practice Files* folder we have used in *Chapter 3 Working with Mixbook*:

The *Sample Pictures* folder, contains the default *Windows* sample pictures:

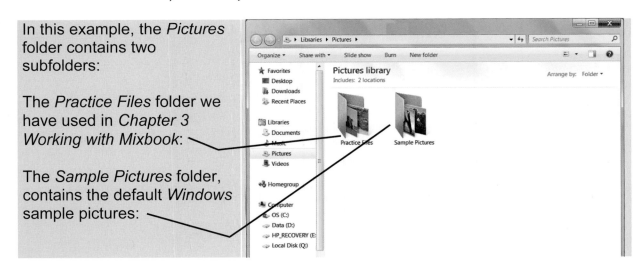

❧ Please note!

You may see more folders on your own computer. If you always use your *Pictures* folder to store your photos, this folder may also contain individual photo files.

This is how to create a new subfolder in the *Pictures* folder:

In *Windows 7*:

 Click New folder

In *Windows Vista*:

 Click Organize ▼, New Folder

In *Windows XP*:

 Click File, New, 📁 Folder

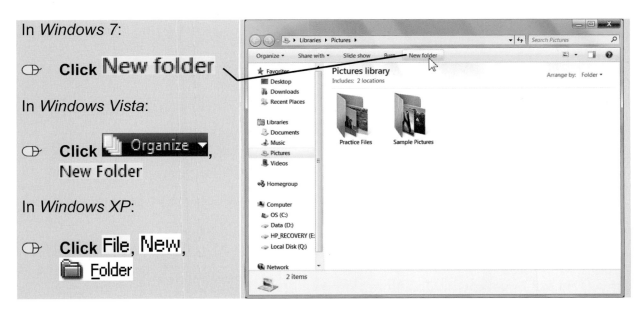

Now a new, empty folder has been added. For now, this folder is still called *New folder*.

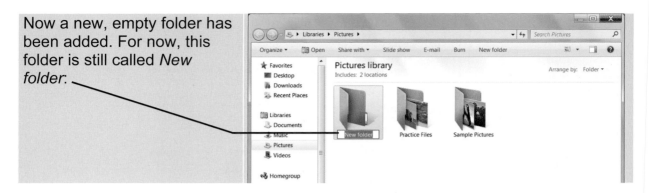

You can enter a name for this new folder right away:

For example, type:
`Pictures for photo book`

Press Enter

Now the folder has a new name. In the following section you are going to copy photos to this folder.

6.2 Copying Photos to the New Folder

It is a good idea to copy the photos you want to use in your photo book to a new folder. This way, the original photos will not be changed or accidentally deleted when you are working in your photo book, or when you are editing them in some way or other.

 Please note!
In this example we have used some sample photos, but if you prefer, you can use your own photos.
If you do not have any photos stored on your computer, you can download the sample photos by visiting **www.visualsteps.com/photobook**
There you will find the practice photos as well as instructions on how to download them to the (*My*) *Pictures* folder.

You can find the sample photos we have used in this example in the *Practice Files* folder. Open this folder:

Double-click

You will see the practice photos. This is how you copy a photo:

In *Windows 7* and *Vista*:

Click a photo

Click Organize ▼

Click Copy

In *Windows XP*:

Click Edit, Copy

Now you can paste the photo into the new folder. You can open the new folder in the folder list shown in the left-hand side of the window:

In *Windows XP*:

☞ **If necessary, click**
   Folders

In *Windows 7* and *Vista*:

☞ **Double-click** Pictures

In *Windows 7* and *XP*:

☞ **Double-click**
   My Pictures

In all *Windows* editions:

☞ **Click**
   Pictures for photo book

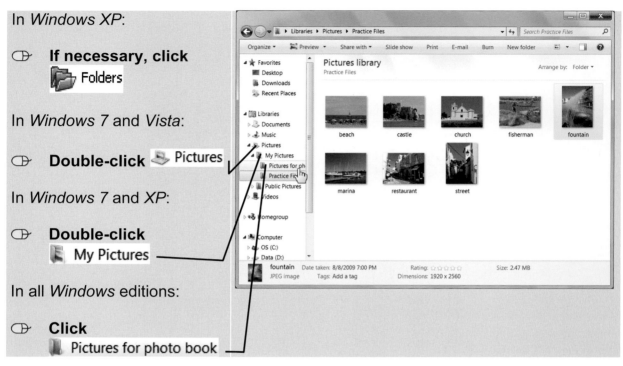

In *Windows 7* and *Vista*:

☞ **Click** Organize ▼

In *Windows XP*:

☞ **Click** Edit

In all *Windows* editions:

☞ **Click** Paste

Now the copied photo has been pasted into the new folder:

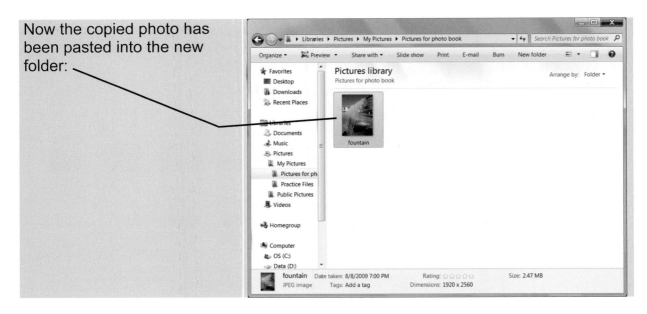

Close the window ℰℰ³

💡 **Tip**

Selecting and copying multiple photos at once
If you want to use more than one photo from the same folder, you can select them all at once. This is how you select a number of consecutive photos:

👆 **Click the first photo**

⌨ **Press**

⬆ Shift

and hold it down

👆 **Click the last photo**

⌨ **Release**

⬆ Shift

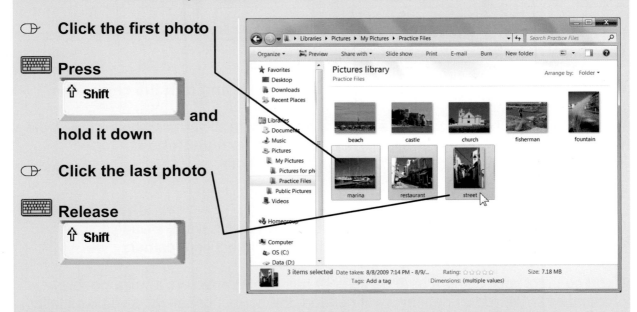

Now the photo in between has also been selected. Next, you can go ahead and copy and paste other photos, just like you learned to do in the previous steps.

- Continue reading on the next page -

You can also select a number of non-consecutive photos. Here is how you do that:

☞ **Click a photo**

Press [Ctrl] **and hold it down**

☞ **Click another photo**

Release [Ctrl]

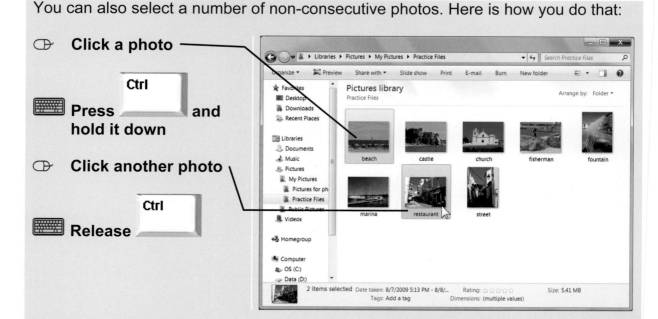

Now both photos have been selected. Continue further and copy and paste other photos until your selection is complete.

6.3 Importing Photos from Your Digital Camera

In *Windows 7, Vista* and *XP* you can use the *Windows Explorer* to import photos from your digital camera.

Connect your digital camera to your computer and turn the camera on

If you don't know how to connect a digital photo camera to your computer, check the website accompanying this book: **www.visualsteps.com/photobook**
There you will find an additional PDF file with instructions.

Please note!

Digital cameras can be connected to computers in various ways. Read your camera's manual, if necessary, to find out how to connect your camera.

If you connect your camera and the camera has been turned on, it will probably be recognized by *Windows* right away. If needed, the correct driver will also be installed.

As soon as your camera has been detected by *Windows*, you may see the *AutoPlay* window:

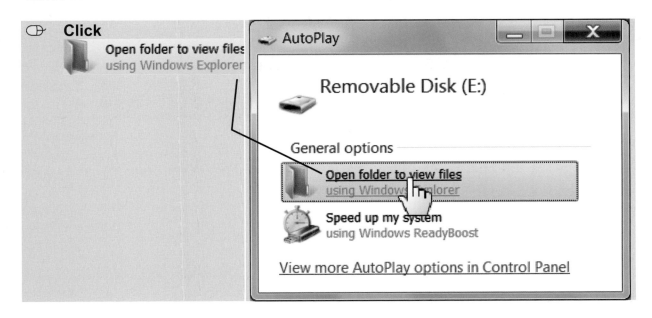

HELP! I do not see this window

If the *AutoPlay* window does not appear on your screen, you can also open the folder in *Windows Explorer*:

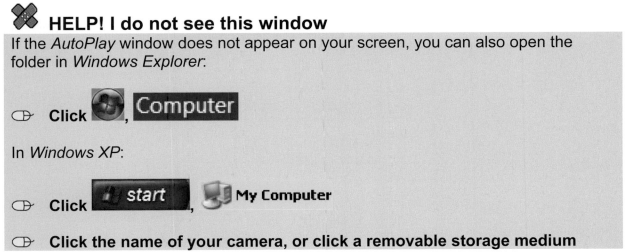

☞ **Click** , **Computer**

In *Windows XP*:

☞ **Click** *start*, 🖥 **My Computer**

☞ **Click the name of your camera, or click a removable storage medium**

The content of your digital camera will be displayed in *Windows Explorer*:

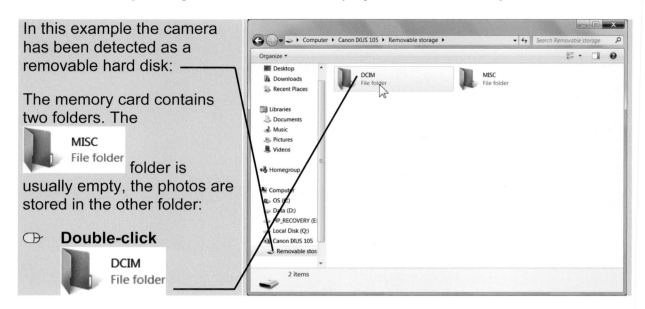

In this example the camera has been detected as a removable hard disk:

The memory card contains two folders. The MISC File folder folder is usually empty, the photos are stored in the other folder:

☞   **Double-click** DCIM File folder

In the DCIM folder you will find one or more folders with photos:

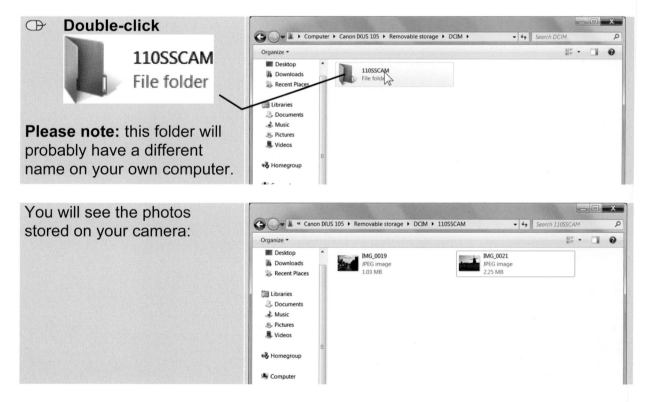

☞   **Double-click** 110SSCAM File folder

Please note: this folder will probably have a different name on your own computer.

You will see the photos stored on your camera:

You can copy these photos to a folder on your computer. This works the same way as copying files between two different folders on your computer.

Previously, you have learned how to copy one or more photos. But you can also copy all the photos at once. This is how to select all of the photos in this folder:

In *Windows 7* and *Vista*:

☞ **Click** Organize ▼

In *Windows XP*:

☞ **Click** Edit

In all editions:

☞ **Click** Select all

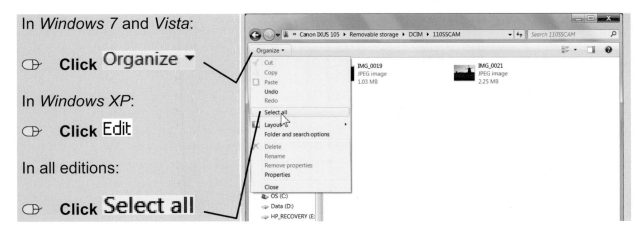

Now all photos have been selected. Next, you can copy the photos:

In *Windows 7* and *Vista*:

☞ **Click** Organize ▼

In *Windows XP*:

☞ **Click** Edit

In all editions:

☞ **Click** Copy

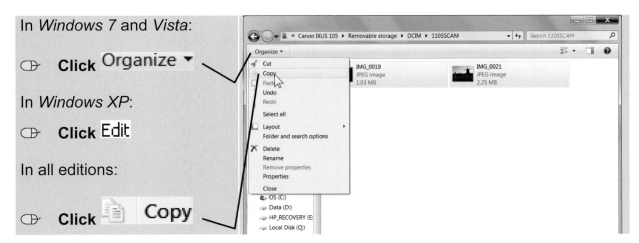

Open the *Pictures* folder:

In *Windows 7* and *Vista*:

☞ **Double-click** Pictures

In *Windows 7*:

☞ **Click** My Pictures

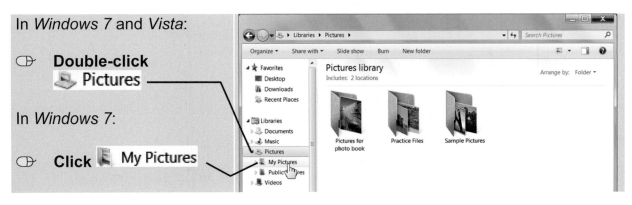

This is what you do in *Windows XP*:

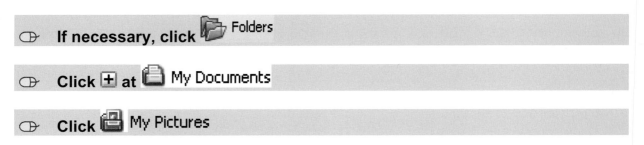

☞ **If necessary, click** 📁 Folders

☞ **Click** ⊞ **at** 📄 My Documents

☞ **Click** 🖼 My Pictures

Now you can paste the photos you copied from the digital camera into the *Pictures* folder:

In *Windows 7* and *Vista*:

☞ **Click** Organize ▾

In *Windows XP*:

☞ **Click** Edit

In all editions:

☞ **Click** 📋 Paste

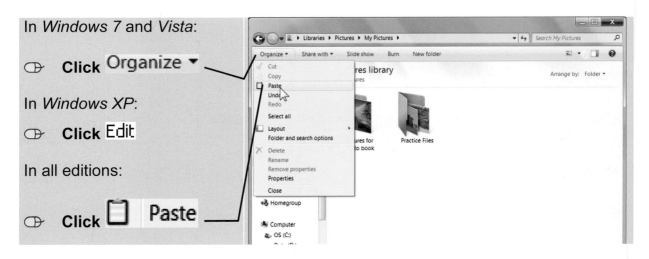

Now the photos from the digital camera have been copied to the *Pictures* folder:

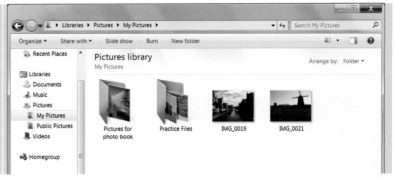

☞ **Close all open windows** ✂³

☞ **Turn your camera off and disconnect it from the computer**

You have now learned how to transfer photos from your digital camera to your computer.

6.4 Connecting the Scanner

If your scanner has a USB connection, you can connect it to your computer. In most cases when you connect a scanner for the first time, whether in *Windows 7*, *Vista* and *XP*, the appropriate driver will also be installed.

 Please note!

However, some scanners require specific driver software that has to be installed first before you connect the scanner to the USB port. Other scanners need to be turned on before or during the installation of the software. Read your scanner's manual and make sure you install your scanner in the proper way. You can also use the *Scanner and Camera Installation Wizard* (see the *Tip* at the end of this chapter).

 HELP! My scanner is still not recognized

If your scanner is not recognized by *Windows*, even though you have used the *Scanner and Camera Installation Wizard*, you can take a look at the manufacturer's website. You may be able to find and download a driver there that is suitable for your version of *Windows*. Or you can visit your local hardware supplier.

☞ **Make sure the scanner has been installed in the correct way**

☞ **Make sure the scanner is turned on**

Some scanners will automatically start the scanning program that goes with the scanner. If this happens with your scanner:

☞ **Close the scanning program**

☞ **Insert a photo into the scanner. The print side of the photo should be placed on the glass bed.**

6.5 Scanning Photos in Windows 7 and Windows Vista

☞ **If necessary, close the window of your scanner** ✇³

In *Windows 7* and *Windows Vista* you can scan documents and photos by using the *Windows Fax and Scan* program:

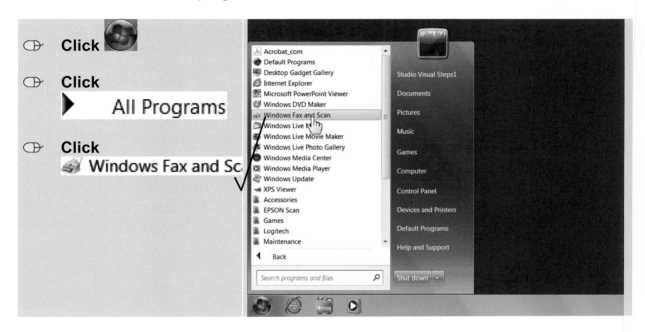

You will see the *Windows Fax and Scan* window. Now you are going to start a new scan:

You will see the *New Scan* window:

By default, the program is set to scan a photo:

Here you can set the color of the photo (color, black and white, or grey tones):

Here you can select the file type for the scanned photo:

By **Resolution (DPI):** you can set the number of dots (Dots Per Inch) the scan should use. You are going to select 1200 dpi:

 Double-click the box

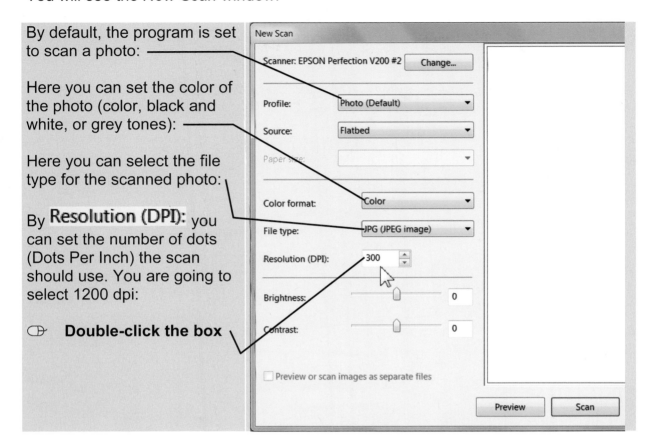

Tip

Scan quality and DPI
The scan quality is expressed in DPI: *Dots Per Inch*. This is also called the *resolution*. Depending on your objective, you can select a setting starting from 100 up to a maximum of 1200 DPI (depending on your scanner).

For instance, if you want to place a photo on your website, the quality does not need to be very high. In that case, 100 DPI will do. If you want to use a regular, 4x6 inch picture in your photo book, a resolution of 400 DPI is sufficient. But if you want to have a photo stretch across a full or double page, it is better to select the highest resolution of 1200 DPI. A 4x6 inch photo that is scanned with a resolution of 1200 DPI will result in a file size of about 3 MB.

First, you are going to make a preview of the scan:

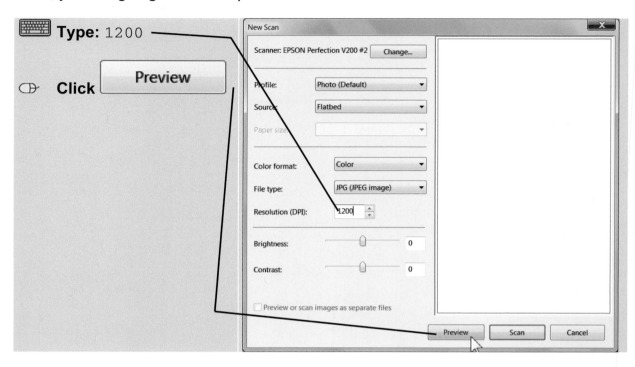

Type: 1200

Click Preview

You will see the preview:

A dotted frame will indicate which area will be scanned. As you can see, a large portion of the white area will also be scanned:

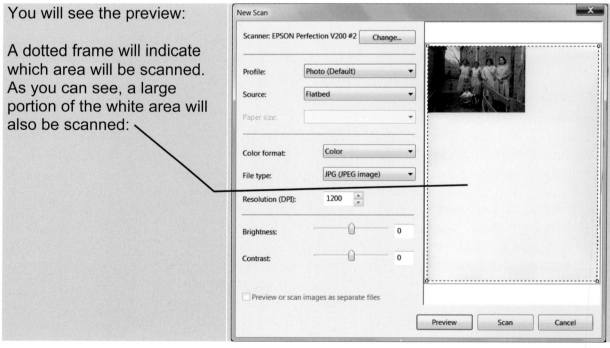

You can still adjust the area that is going to be scanned:

⊕ **Position the mouse pointer on a corner handle of the dotted frame** ———

⊕ **Drag the corner handle until you have reached the desired size**

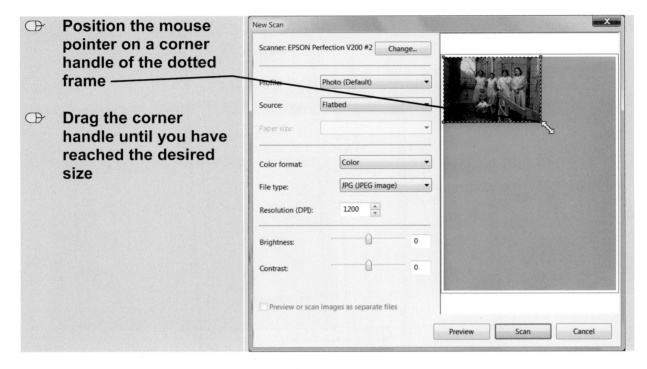

If you are satisfied with your adjustments, you can start the scan:

⊕ **Click**

Scan

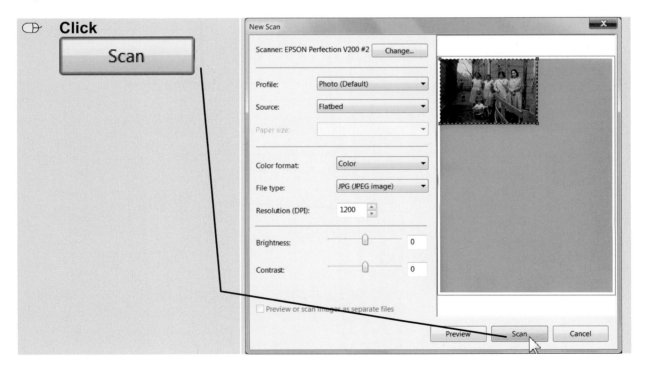

Now the photo will be scanned:

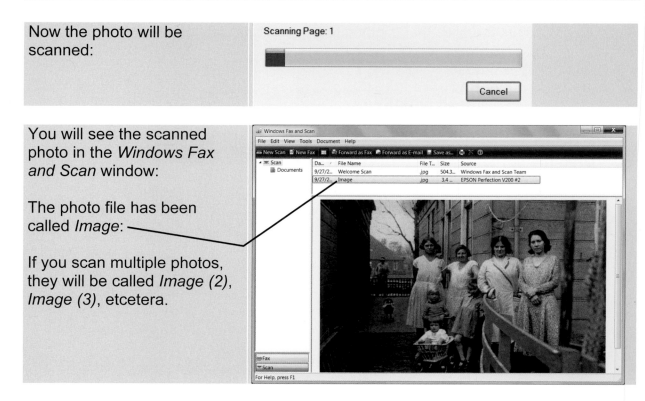

You will see the scanned photo in the *Windows Fax and Scan* window:

The photo file has been called *Image*:

If you scan multiple photos, they will be called *Image (2)*, *Image (3)*, etcetera.

The scanned photo has been stored in the *Scanned Documents* folder. This is a subfolder of the *Documents* folder. You can navigate to this folder now:

☞ **Click** [icon], **Documents**

The *Documents* folder will be opened:

☞ **Double-click**

[folder icon] **Scanned Documen**
            File folder

You may see additional folders and files than the ones shown here.

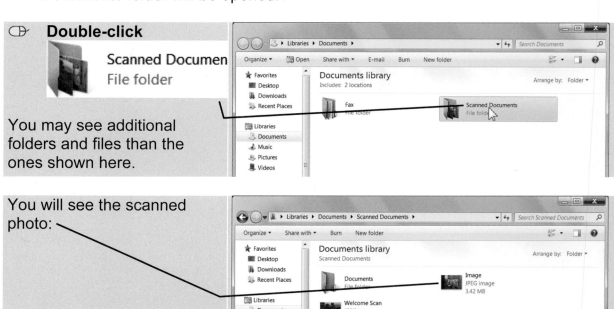

You will see the scanned photo:

Now you can copy the scanned photo, in the same way you copied the other photos earlier.

 Tip

Different name
Before copying or moving the scanned photo, it is a good idea to rename it first and give it a more obvious or useful name, so that you will easily recognize it later on. Here is to do that:

☞ **Click the photo**

☞ **Click** Organize ▾, Rename

⌨ **Type a new name for the photo**

☞ **Close all open windows** ✿³

6.6 Scanning Photos in Windows XP

In *Windows XP* you can scan photos by using the *Scanner and Camera Wizard.*

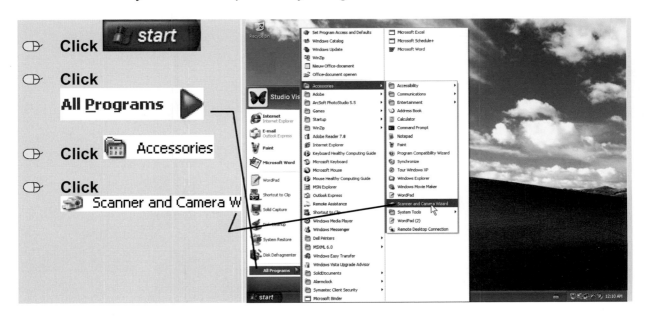

In the *Select Device* window you need to select the scanner:

☞ **Click your scanner**

Now you will see the first window of the *Scanner and Camera Wizard*:

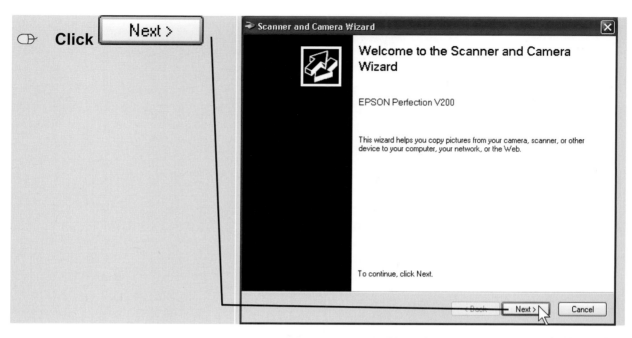

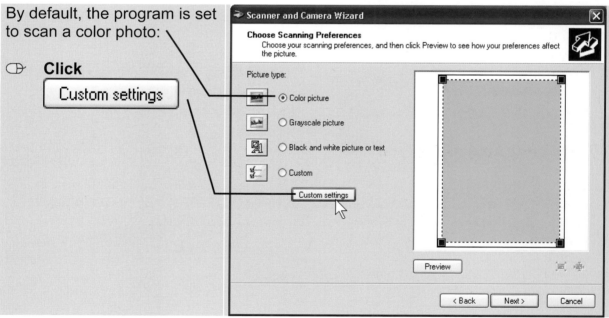

The *Properties* window will be opened:

By Resolution (DPI): you can set the number of dots (Dots Per Inch) that will be used for the scan. You are going to select 1200 DPI:

☞ **Double-click the box**

⌨ **Type:** 1200

☞ **Click** OK

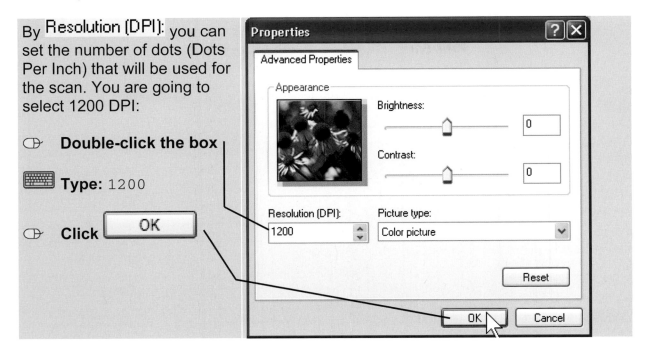

💡 **Tip**

Scan quality and DPI

The scan quality is expressed in DPI: *Dots Per Inch*. This is also called the *resolution*. Depending on your objective, you can select a setting starting from 100 up to a maximum of 1200 DPI (depending on your scanner).

For instance, if you want to place a photo on your website, the quality does not need to be very high. In that case, 100 DPI will do. If you want to use a regular, 4x6 inch picture in your photo book, a resolution of 400 DPI is sufficient. But if you want to have a photo stretch across a full or double page, it is better to select the highest resolution of 1200 DPI. A 4x6 inch photo that is scanned with a resolution of 1200 DPI will result in a file size of about 3 MB.

First, you are going to make a preview of the scan:

☞ **Click** Preview

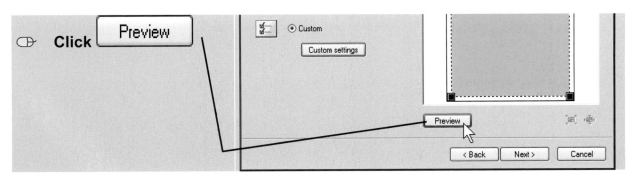

You will see the preview:

A dotted frame indicates the area that will be scanned. As you can see, at the bottom a small white border is also included in the scan:

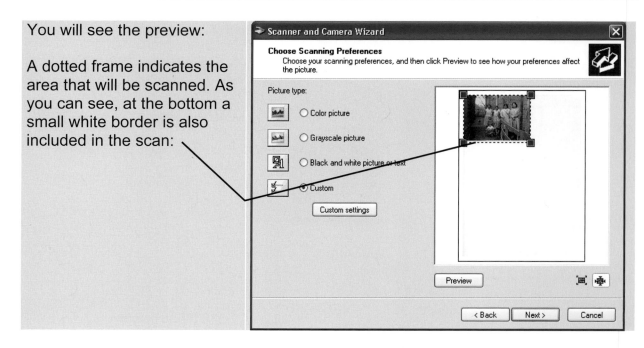

You can still adjust the area that is going to be scanned:

Position the mouse pointer on a corner handle of the dotted frame

Drag the corner handle until you have reached the desired size

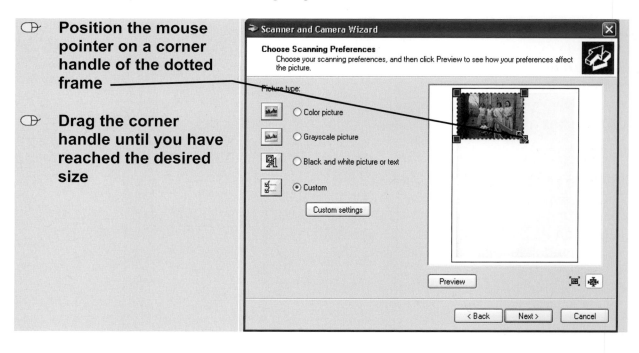

If you are satisfied with your adjustments, you can continue with the next window of the wizard:

Click **Next >**

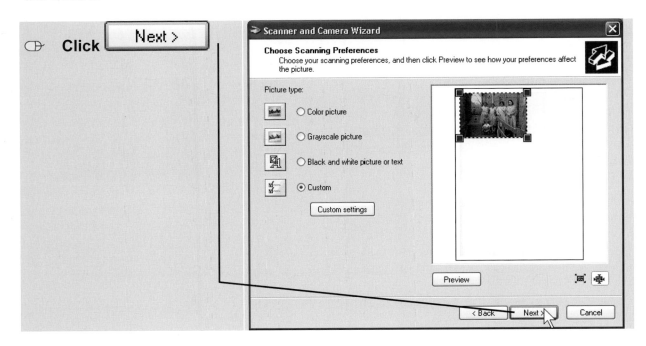

Now you can enter a name for the photos you are going to scan. The photos that you scan in consecutive order will receive the same name, appended by a number in sequence.

For example, type:
Scan

By default, the JPG file format is selected:

You do not need to change that.

The scanned photos will be stored in the *Scan* folder within the *My Pictures* folder:

Click **Next >**

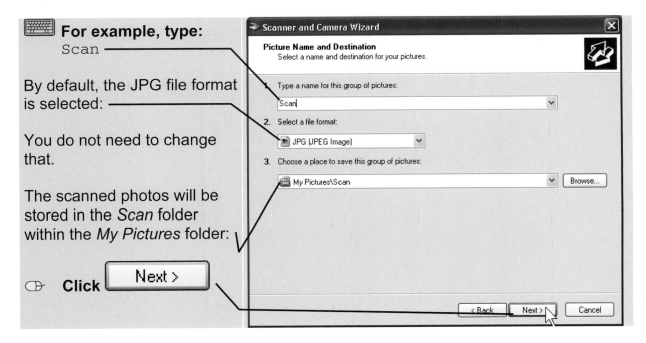

The photo will be scanned:

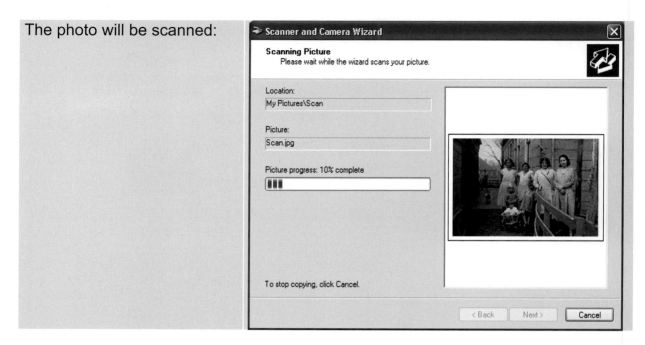

Now the wizard will ask you what to do with the photos. You are going to choose to stop working with these pictures:

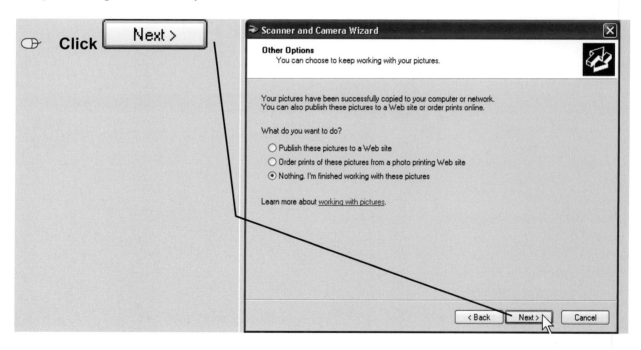

Now you can close the wizard:

In the bottom of the window:

👉 **Click** Finish

The *Scan* folder in the *My Pictures* folder will open automatically:

You will see the scanned photo:

The photo file has also been called *Scan*:

If you scan multiple photos, they will be called *Scan 001*, *Scan 002*, etcetera.

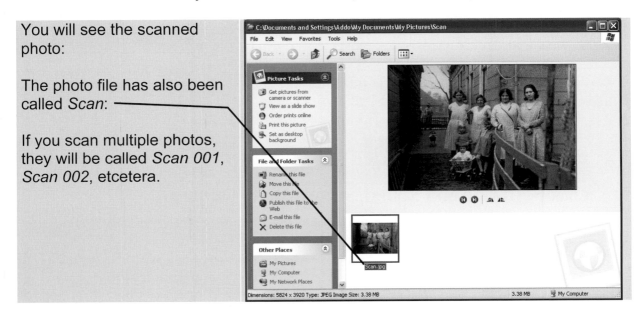

Now you can copy the scanned photo, in the same way as you copied the other photos earlier.

💡 **Tip**

Different name

Before copying or moving the scanned photo, it is a good idea to rename it first and give it a more obvious or useful name, so that you will easily recognize it later on. Here is to do that:

👉 **Click the photo**

👉 **Click** File, Rename

⌨ **Type a new name for the photo**

👉 **Close all open windows** ³

In this chapter you have learned how to collect and organize the photos you will need for your photo book.

6.7 Tips

 Tip

Scanner and Camera Wizard
In *section 6.3 Importing Photos from Your Digital Camera* you can read how to transfer photos from your digital camera to your computer.
If *Windows* does not immediately recognize your camera, you can use the *Scanner and Camera Installation Wizard* in *Windows Vista* and *XP*. This wizard will help you install the correct drivers for older scanners and cameras that are not automatically recognized by *Windows*.
These driver installation problems seldom occur in *Windows 7*, so we will not discuss them in this book.

This is how you start the *Scanner and Camera Installation Wizard* in *Windows Vista*:

☞ **Click**

☞ **Click** Hardware and Sound, Scanners and Cameras

☞ **Click** Add Device...

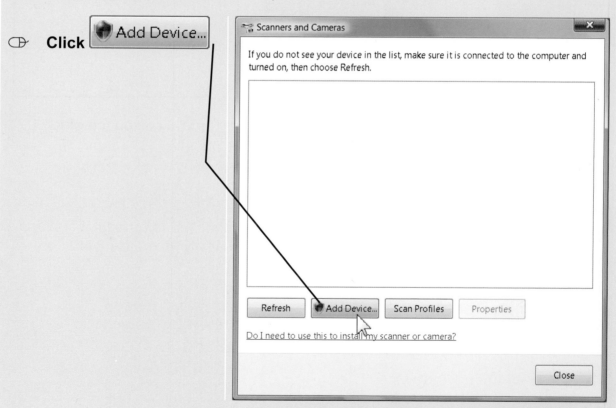

- Continue reading on the next page -

Now your screen will turn dark and you will need to give permission to continue:

☞ **Give permission to continue**

↪ **Click** [Next >]

☞ **Go through the various steps of the wizard and follow the instructions in each window**

If you have a CD ROM disk that contains the driver software that goes with your scanner, the wizard will ask you to insert that CD.

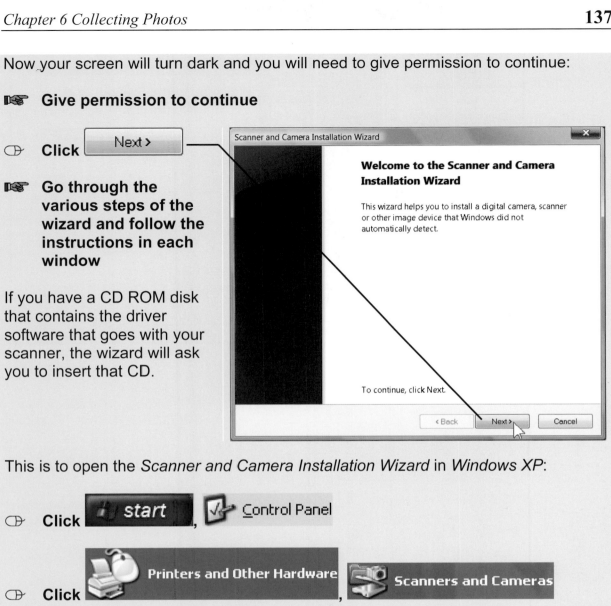

This is to open the *Scanner and Camera Installation Wizard* in *Windows XP*:

↪ **Click** [start] , [Control Panel]

↪ **Click** [Printers and Other Hardware] , [Scanners and Cameras]

↪ **Click** Add an imaging device

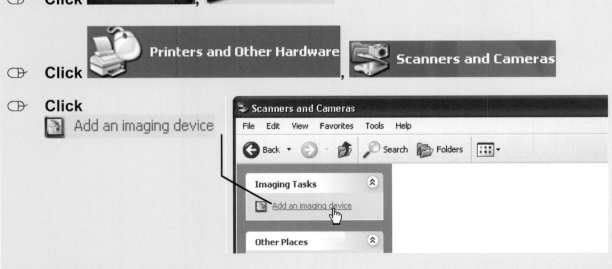

- Continue reading on the next page -

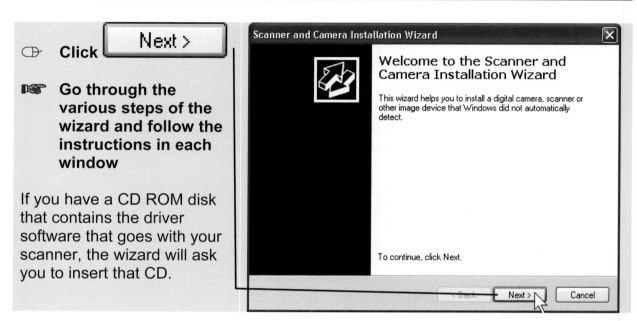

Click [**Next >**]

☞ **Go through the various steps of the wizard and follow the instructions in each window**

If you have a CD ROM disk that contains the driver software that goes with your scanner, the wizard will ask you to insert that CD.

7. Create a Vacation Photo Book

Many people enjoy their vacation time. It is often the highlight of the year. Are you someone who looks forward to your vacation, months in advance? Do you like to reminisce about the places you have been to or do you find yourself thinking about some of the things you did in a previous vacation? Then creating a vacation photo book may be just the right thing for you!

In this album you can collect your nicest vacation photos and combine them with a story. You can make your story as expansive as you like: short captions to go with the pictures or a longer story in which you describe your adventures in full. You can even add an anecdote here and there to give your book some humor.

This chapter will give you plenty of ideas on how to compose your own vacation story. You might want to start by making a kind of diary, jotting down the things you did each day. You can then take one or more of the highlights of your travels and discuss them more fully. There are lots of ideas in this chapter to get you started, both for the content of your story as well as for the design of your photo book.

In this chapter you can read about:

- using an action plan for writing your travel story;
- choosing a logical structure for your travel story;
- finding inspiration for the contents and design of your own photo book, by looking at the examples.

 Please note!

This chapter offers several examples of titles that you can use for your own vacation story. But don't let these limit you. You can make up your own titles as you go. You can skip some headings, or rename them and add new headings wherever that seems appropriate.

 Please note!

The length of your descriptive text can vary widely.
In our examples we have restricted the length per topic to cover one or two pages. But, you can use more than two pages per topic if you desire. You can even fill an entire page with just text. It is entirely up to you.

Please note!

In each example shown in this chapter, we include the name of the photo book software it was made with as well as the formatting options used. Photo book software providers continue to improve their programs. It may occur that a particular background, template, frame or font is no longer available in the version of software you are using.

7.1 Action Plan

If you want to write a travel story or any other type of story, for that matter, you can follow a fixed action plan:

Step 1   Think about your story and write down some keywords that sum up what you want to tell.

Step 2   Collect the photos you want to use in your book and store them in a separate folder (see *Chapter 6 Collecting Photos*).

Step 3   Open the photo book software you are going to use, create a new project and select the desired format (see *Chapter 3 Working with Mixbook*).

Step 4   Create a cover for your book, if you wish (see *Chapter 3 Working with Mixbook*).

Step 5   Think about the type of image you want to project on your page and then select a suitable background in the photo book software (see *Chapter 3 Working with Mixbook*).

Step 6   Add text and photos to the page.

Step 7   Modify the layout: select a suitable format for the photo boxes and text boxes on the page. Select a font and font size for the text. If you want, you can also add frames, templates and clip art. (see *Chapter 3 Working with Mixbook*).

Repeat steps 5, 6, and 7 for all the pages in your book.

Step 8   Check all the pages, paying close attention to the formatting, headings and spelling (see *Chapter 4 Writing Tips* and *Chapter 5 Formatting Tips*).

Step 9   Send the album to the print service.

In the following section you will find more examples and some ideas for step 6.

 Tip

Short/long texts
If you are planning to write short pieces of text and want to use a lot of pictures, you can start using the photo book software right away.

If you want to write longer stories, it may be easier to write the full story in a text editing program first. Then later, you can insert the text into the photo book software. You can do this by copying and pasting the text into the book (see *Chapter 3 Working with Mixbook*).

7.2 The Structure of Your Story

There are many different ways to tell a story about a vacation. If you have travelled a great deal, a day-to-day account might make an interesting book. You can describe the events on a single day in chronological order.

But try to confine yourself to the most interesting activities and events. People who read your book do not necessarily want to know at what time you got up each day, and what you had for breakfast. But it will be interesting to read about your activities on a specific day:

- where were you that day?
- what did you do there? Relax, shop, do some sightseeing, sports?
- which sights, monuments or museums have you visited?
- did you see or do something special on that particular day?

You can use as many words as you want for writing about your daily experiences. If you need more space to write about some specific activity, you can expand your text. But you can also confine the text to simple captions accompanying each photo, describing the subject in the photo and the location where it was taken.

Program: Mixbook | Theme Tropical Cruise | Standard background, two page spread | Standard white frame | Font: Cooper Black (title), Tahoma (text)

An example documenting a traveler's experiences day by day. There will most likely be days where you have a lot stories, and other days where nothing much happened. Add pages and photos where needed to depict the events and experiences that seemed significant to you.

  Make a chronological overview of all the days of your journey

  Use keywords to describe your activities on various days

  Collect photos and sort them by date taken or activity

  Write a (short) piece of text for each day

If you intend to write a day-to-day account of your fortnight's stay in a Spanish apartment, you will soon run out of fresh topics. In this case, it is better to choose a number of different themes and describe these. For example, you can build your book by using the following examples of titles and headings.

➥ Please note!

The titles in this chapter are just meant to inspire you and give you some ideas. You are not obliged to structure your photo book in exactly the same way, or use the same titles. We do not pretend to give a complete overview: you can add or remove titles that fit your story better.

Where Was the Journey Headed?

Start your story by giving a brief description of your destination. If you spent your vacation at the beach, describe where you were staying. If you were travelling around, then describe the country or continent you were visiting. You can write down this description in your own words, or use a description from a brochure from your travel agency or by the website where you booked your vacation.

 Tip

Use the Internet
The Internet is a great source of information for all sorts of travels and destinations.

Consider these sites:
- the travel agency's website
- *Wikipedia*
- the tourist information website from the specific city or country

After adding a simple description of the place or destination, you can expand your story further with more information. What about this:
- who chose the destination?
- have you visited this place before? If yes, how long have you been visiting this place?
- why did you go to this place? Have you always wanted to visit this country/city? Does your family live there? Or was it sheer coincidence, for instance because you won a travel voucher in a competition?

☞ **Describe your travel destination**

A description can be accompanied by one or more pictures. Select photos that provide information about the destination. For example, a town view, a city sign, a seascape or a landscape.

☞ **Look for one or more matching photos**

You can choose to write your story with a text editing program, or directly in your photo book. If you are going to use a text editor, it is useful to make a note of the folder where you have stored the photos you want to use. If you include the file names or numbers right away, you will not need to look them up when you start compiling your photo book.

Like this, for example:

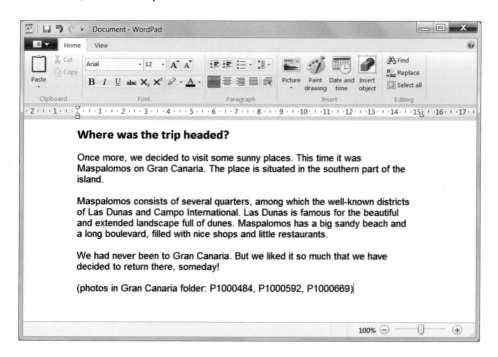

If you enter your text directly into your photo book, the page might start off looking something like this:

Program:
Mixbook

Background:
Shells2.jpg

Template applied to all photos

Font: Arial

Did you travel with anyone else?

It is a good idea to tell your readers who you were with on the trip, especially if you were traveling with a large group of people.

☞ Find a photo where the whole traveling party is portrayed

If you do not have a picture in which everyone is represented, you can combine several different pictures together.

☞ Describe who is in the photo(s)

Do you expect other people to view your book, besides the people who were part of the traveling group? Then it is a good idea to tell your public about the mutual relationship. Was it family, friends or colleagues? If there was a specific reason for this group of people to go on holiday together, tell the viewer about it. Like this, for example:

WHO JOINED US?

On the occasion of Grandmother's 70th birthday we have taken a trip with Grandma, Hank, the kids, their partners, and all the grandchildren.

Program: Shutterfly

Theme Travel - Hit the Road

Standard background

Font:
Rosewood (title)
Backtalk (text)

Program: My Publisher

Own photo as a background

Font: Broadway

The Itinerary

If you have made a tour, you can insert the itinerary at the beginning of your book. Like this, for instance:

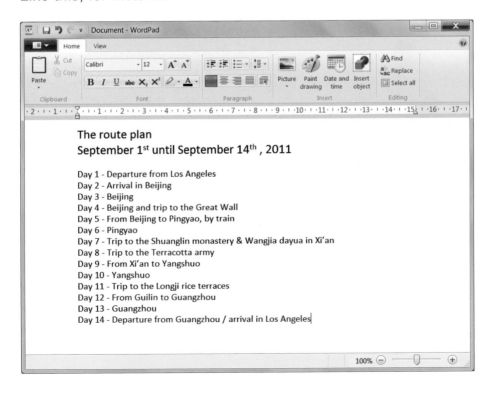

☞ **Type your travel itinerary**

 Tip

Use the Tab key

Tab

Use the _____ key to separate the days from the descriptions. This way, everything will be neatly aligned. If you use the space bar to do this, the text might not be properly aligned.

HELP! The Tab key does not seem to function properly

In most of the programs for creating photo books, the Tab key does not work properly.

Ctrl   Tab

Instead, you may be able to use the combination of: _____ + _____ keys.

☞ **Find a photo that matches the travel itinerary**

For example, what type of transportation did you use for this trip? Did you travel by car, camper, train, bus or boat? If you were on an organized trip, perhaps you have a photo with a logo from the tour operator or a photo of the tour guide, for instance. Or even a photo of the travel agency's presentation on a bulletin board at the hotel.

The Luggage

Your luggage can also be a nice topic to dedicate a page to in your book:
- did it take very long to pack your bags?
- were the suitcases terribly heavy? Who had the most luggage?
- did everything fit into the car/caravan/camper/saddle-bags/backpack?
- which things did you forget to pack? And your companions?
- what was the weirdest item that someone in your group wanted to bring along?

☞ **Write a piece on the topic of packing your bags and luggage and find one or more matching photos**

The Departure

You might be able to fill an entire page with an account of your departure. Did you take some nice pictures at the train station or airport, or at home, when you were saying goodbye?

Just write about what is happening in your photos. If something unusual happened, or things did not go according to plan, you might also be able to expand your story a bit further:

- were there any delays? How long did you have to wait and what caused the delay?
- did somebody arrive at the very last minute?
- did you have to turn around and go back home because someone had forgotten something important? Or they had to make sure appliances were turned off?
- did you have trouble at the customs office, for instance because someone was carrying too many liquid substances in his or her luggage?

☞ **Write a story about your departure and find one or more matching photos**

 Tip
Combining topics
You can also combine the topics mentioned above and write both stories on a single page.

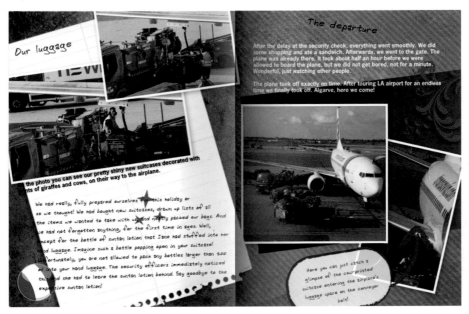

Program:
Mixbook

Theme Europe
Backpacking Trip

Fonts: Domestic
Manners and New
Gothic Std

The Journey

Naturally, there are lots of different ways to travel to a particular destination. By car, camper, train, airplane, boat, bicycle, among others. All of these will have one thing in common: they are bound to supply more ideas for your story. Write about how you travelled.

In general:
- did you make any intermediate stops in interesting places? What did you do or see there, did anything particular or unusual happen there?
- did you spend the night somewhere along the way?
- did you change over to another plane/train/boat?
- did you see or experience anything special on the way?
- how did you spend your time while travelling? Chatting, checking the map, playing games, listening to music or watching a movie?
- how did the kids behave during the trip? What did they do? Which games did they play, did they fight or were they well-behaved?

If you traveled by airplane, you could answer these questions:
- were you comfortable on the plane? Did you have a window seat, or along the aisle?
- how long did the flight take?
- did you talk to your fellow passengers?
- did you have to transfer to your final destination? How did it go?

Michael had a window seat. He was able to take beautiful pictures when we flew over the Atlantic.

For the rest, the flight was uneventful. We had already seen the movie and the food was nice!

Program:
Picaboo

Own photo as a background across two pages

Frame applied to the photos

Font:
Sandra Regular

If you traveled by car, you could answer these questions:
*   did you drive along any special sights?
*   was it easy to find your destination?
*   were there any traffic jams?
*   did you have any car trouble or an accident along the way?
*   how did the kids in the backseat behave? What did they do to spend their time?

If you traveled by train, you could answer these questions:
*   how long did the journey take?
*   did you talk to the other passengers in your compartment?
*   did you sleep in a berth on a night train? How did you like that?

☞   **Write a story about your journey and find one or more matching photos**

Arrival at the Camping Site

When you are in the act of setting up a tent, or a caravan at a camping site, you may feel that finally your camping trip has gotten started. Hopefully, this will go quickly and smoothly, and leave you some time to explore your surroundings afterwards. But even if things do not go exactly as planned, you will always be left with a great story to tell in your book.

In general:
*   was your camping spot anything like the spot you had booked in advance? Did it turn out better than you expected? Or were you disappointed?
*   what did your camping location look like? Was it in the shade, by the sea, close to the pool, or was it a nice secluded spot?
*   was it easy to reach the campground?
*   did the other campers help you set up the tent or set up the caravan?
*   meanwhile, what did the kids do?

The tent:
*   did you manage to set up the tent on the first try?
*   did you bring along all the necessary parts, such as the pegs, spikes or ropes?

The caravan:
*   did you manage to park the caravan into its place without any trouble?
*   did you bring along all the necessary parts for the awning?

At Last, the Campground

After a long journey we finally arrived in Privas. In the village we had to ask somebody for directions to the campground because there were several other camping sites in the area. Our camping site was very quiet and rural, right in the middle of nature. The camp manager pointed us to a pretty spot under the trees, overlooking the valley.

Our kids immediately found new friends in Anne and Sam, two children who were camped nearby. When we started setting up the tent, Wesley and Jessica instantly disappeared. Anne and Sam took them on a trip to explore the campground. They had already been there for a couple of days, so they knew their way around.

It did not take long to set up the tent, thank goodness; we got the hang of it right away. It was very tempting afterwards to stop right there and then and sit down with a glass of wine in hand and enjoy the view. But we decided to unpack first and put everything in its place. Now we could really start enjoying the holidays!

☞ **Write a story about your arrival at the camping site and find one or more matching photos**

Arrival at the Apartment / Hotel Room

If you have booked a fully organized trip, including overnight stays in a hotel or an apartment, it is always a surprise to find out what your accommodation actually looks like. Does the hotel look like the glossy photos in your travel brochure or is everything very different?

You can expand your story further by including information about your lodgings. If you have some good pictures of your hotel or apartment, a brief description will suffice. But if you have other stories to tell regarding your accommodation, you can elaborate a bit more. For instance, like this:

- what was your first impression of the hotel or apartment building? Was the travel agency's description accurate or was the accommodation completely different?
- how many rooms did you rent and how were the members of your group spread over these rooms?
- were there things that did not satisfy you? For example, were there any broken items or were the rooms not clean enough? Or, on the contrary, was everything much prettier than you expected?
- was the accommodation close to the beach or the pool?

Program:
Picaboo

Standard background photo theme Travel

Shadow applied to all photos

Font: Sandra Regular

☞ **Write a story about the accommodation and find one or more matching photos**

Enjoying the Beach or the Pool

Did you have a good time at the beach or in the swimming pool in a warm country? Then you should write about it in your book. If you took a lot of nice pictures, you will be able to fill a few pages with these. Describe what the pictures are all about, or expand on some of the things you did:

- what did the beach or swimming pool look like?
- was it very crowded?
- was the water cold or too warm?
- did your kids play with other children?
- what kind of games did they play?
- were there any organized activities? Who organized these? Did you and/or your children participate?

Especially in the mornings, the swimming pool was really quiet. What a luxury to have the whole pool to yourself! We enjoyed reading our books and diving into the water once in a while. At the end of the afternoon it got a bit more crowded, when everyone got back from the beach. But by that time we had had enough sunshine and we gave up our stretchers to the new visitors.

Program: Picaboo

Own photo as a background

Font: Arial

 Tip

Title
It is not necessary to add a title for each piece of text. Text alone can be just as nice.

☞ **Write a story about the beach and/or swimming pool and find one or more matching photos**

Going Out for a Nice Dinner

Your book will be more complete if it includes a story about a pleasant dinner you had with your travelling party or with new friends you made during your vacation.

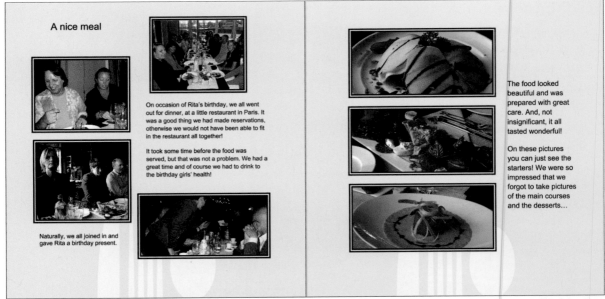

Program: Blurb Booksmart | Standard background across two pages | Border applied to the photos | Font: Arial

Tell the viewer about the people you had dinner with and where you went for dinner. Was there some special occasion, such as a birthday or wedding anniversary? Maybe you can write something about the restaurant, or about the meal you had.

☞ **Write a story about a pleasant dinner and find one or more matching photos**

All the Things We Have Seen!

The Excursion To…

The Day Trip To …

Excursions and other day trips are often an essential part of a vacation. Was this vacation more about cultural pursuits than about relaxing and getting a suntan? You will surely be able to fill a number of pages with photos and descriptions of the places you visited. For instance, try to answer the following questions:

- which place did you visit?
- what is this place known for?
- did you go there by yourself or as part of an organized trip?
- which places of interest did you visit, for example, museums, monuments, churches, etcetera?
- what was the highlight of the trip for you? What impressed you the most?

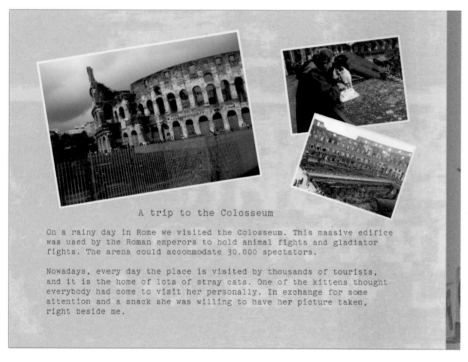

A trip to the Colosseum

On a rainy day in Rome we visited the Colosseum. This massive edifice was used by the Roman emperors to hold animal fights and gladiator fights. The arena could accommodate 30.000 spectators.

Nowadays, every day the place is visited by thousands of tourists, and it is the home of lots of stray cats. One of the kittens thought everybody had come to visit her personally. In exchange for some attention and a snack she was willing to have her picture taken, right beside me.

Program:
Shutterfly

Theme Travel - Hit the Road

Standard background

Font: Pica

☞ **Write one or more stories about excursions or day trips and collect photos to match the stories**

Sports Activities!

Perhaps your vacation was more about sports than about art and cultural activities. Hiking, skiing, skating, cycling, mountain biking, horse riding, mountain climbing, abseiling, playing tennis, playing volleyball, you name it. All these activities can form a crucial part of the book in which you tell the story of your vacation.

Sports activities!

Michael and Edward did not miss any opportunity to engage in a sports competition. Table tennis alongside the pool, throwing a ball inside the pool, and even a horse race at the fair, which was the highlight of the day. The horses are still catching their breath.

Program: Shutterfly

Standard background

Frame applied to all photos

Font: Zalderdash

Just as with all other topics, you can elaborate as much as you like while describing your activities. You can use the following question to describe your sports activities:
- what did you do?
- with whom?
- where?
- independently or in an organized group?
- did you need to get acquainted with the sport there and then or were you already experienced at it?
- who were the best and the worst competitors in your group or the quickest and the slowest?
- any special occurrences?

☞ **Write one or more stories about sports activities and collect matching photos**

Tip

View large examples
You can view larger examples of the pages in this book by visiting the website that accompanies the book: **www.visualsteps.com/photobook**

New Friends

Lifelong Friends!

Have you made some new friends while on vacation? Children, especially, are very quick at making new friends with other kids the same age. Sometimes friendships do not last beyond the vacation, but other times vacation acquaintances become lifelong friends. Whatever the case, these new friends deserve a place in your vacation story book.

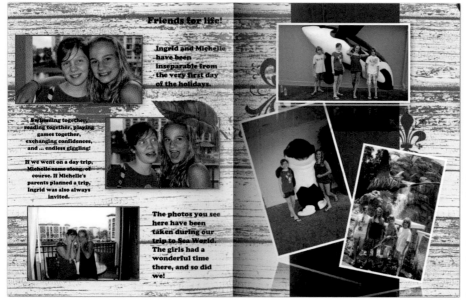

Program:
Mixbook

Theme Europe
Backpacking Trip

Standard background pattern across two pages

Various frames, reflections and stickers applied

Font: Cooper Black

Here are a few things to think about before you start writing the story of your child's new friend:

- where, when and how did your child meet the new friend?
- what is his or her name and where does he or she come from?
- what sorts of things did they do together?
- did they keep in touch after the vacation?

Of course you may also have made new friends yourself. Then you can answer the same questions regarding your own new friends.

☞   **Write a story about your (or your children's) new friends and collect matching photos**

The Journey Home

Alas, everything has to come to an end and so does your wonderful vacation. The bags are packed once more and you are heading home. To complete the story of your vacation, add a page telling about the journey going back home.

You can fill this page with photos you took along the way. You can add extra text to the description of these photos by telling an anecdote on something that occurred during this trip.

The journey back

First, from
Termini railway
station in Rome
to the airport,
by train.

Check in, go past the
customs, have a look in
the tax-free shops,
have a sandwich.

And before you
know it you have
reached the USA
again!

Program:
Blurb

No background

Font:
Simpson (title)
Courier New (text)

7.3 Your Own Photo Book

Hopefully, the sample titles and headings in the previous sections have sufficiently inspired you to start writing your own story. You can expand your travel story as much as you want:

- you can leave out the titles that do not apply to your story
- you can add extra titles for different activities, or special places and events

You can decide for yourself how much text you want to add to each topic. It may be enough just to add a caption to go along with all your photos. But there is no one stopping you from filling an entire page with text when you have something significant or interesting to tell about your journey. In this respect, the photo book software does not impose any restrictions.

 Tip

Read back
Take time once in a while to read over what you have written. You may decide to rephrase an item here and there or add extra lines to your story.

Finally, if you are satisfied with the contents of your book, you can send it to the print service and pay for it. In *Chapter 3 Working with Mixbook* you can read how to do this.

Notes

Write your notes down here.

8. Create a Wedding Day Book

Wedding days are popular topics of conversation, even days afterwards. If you create a photo book about the wedding day of one of your loved ones, the story and the photos can help to ensure that everybody remembers this beautiful day.

In the book you can combine the prettiest wedding day pictures with your own story. You can elaborate as much as you want: short captions to accompany the photos, or a longer account describing all the details of the ceremony and the festivities. You can even include some funny anecdotes here and there! In this chapter we will try to inspire you by presenting various ideas for the contents as well as for the design of your book.

In this chapter you can:

- read about the action plan for creating a story about a wedding day;
- read how to compose your story;
- get some ideas for the contents and layout of your story, by looking at the examples.

 Please note!

This chapter offers several examples of titles that you can use for your own wedding day story. But of course you are not obliged to use all of these titles. You can skip some of them, rename them and add your own titles or headings as you go.

 Please note!

The length of your descriptive text can vary widely.
In our examples we have restricted the length per topic to cover one or two pages. But, you can use more than two pages per topic if you desire. You can even fill an entire page with just text. It is entirely up to you.

 Please note!

In each example shown in this chapter, we include the name of the photo book software it was made with as well as the formatting options used. Photo book software providers continue to improve their programs. It may occur that a particular background, template, frame or font is no longer available in the version of software you are using.

8.1 Action Plan

If you want to create a book about a wedding day, or another important event, you can follow a fixed action plan:

Step 1   Think about your story and write down some keywords that sum up what you want to tell.

Step 2   Collect the photos you want to use in your book and store them in a separate folder (see *Chapter 6 Collecting Photos*).

Step 3   Open the photo book software you are going to use, create a new project and select the desired format (see *Chapter 3 Working with Mixbook*).

Step 4   Create a cover for your book, if you wish (see *Chapter 3 Working with Mixbook*).

Step 5   Think about the type of image you want to project on your page and then select a suitable background in the photo book software (see *Chapter 3 Working with Mixbook*).

Step 6   Add text and photos to the page.

Step 7   Modify the layout: select a suitable format for the photo boxes and text boxes on the page. Select a font and font size for the text. If you want, you can also add frames, templates and clip art. (see *Chapter 3 Working with Mixbook*).

Repeat steps 5, 6, and 7 for all the pages in your book.

Step 8   Check all the pages, paying close attention to the formatting, headings and spelling (see *Chapter 4 Writing Tips* and *Chapter 5 Formatting Tips*).

Step 9   Send the album to the print service.

In the following section you will find more examples and some ideas for step 6.

 Tip

Short/long texts
If you are planning to write short pieces of text and want to use a lot of pictures, you can start using the photo book software right away.
If you want to write longer stories, it may be easier to write the full story in a text editing program first. Then later, you can insert the text into the photo book software. You can do this by copying and pasting the text into the book (see *Chapter 3 Working with Mixbook*).

8.2 The Structure of Your Wedding Story

If you are going to tell a wedding day story, a chronological account would be the most logical option. For example, you can start by describing the way the couple met for the first time. You can make the text in your book as lengthy as you want. If writing comes easy to you, you can use longer pieces of text in your book, including descriptions and anecdotes. If you do not want to use long texts, you can confine yourself to brief descriptions of the subjects in the photos, alternated with a few longer stories. You can compose your story by using the examples of titles and headings below.

 Please note!

The titles in this chapter are just meant to inspire you and give you some ideas. Of course, you are not obliged to structure your album in exactly the same way, or use the same titles. We do not pretend to give a complete overview: you can add or remove titles that fit your story better.

The Encounter

Love at First Sight?

The First Kiss

Courtship

Start your story with a brief description of how the bride and groom first met. Maybe you still have some photos from that period, which show us what the couple looked like at the time. Naturally, these could also be individual photos of the bride and groom, they do not need to be together.

For instance, you could write about:
- where did the bride and groom meet for the first time?
- how old were they at that time?
- what did they think of each other? Did they hate each other, did the sparks start to fly only after years of friendship? Or was it love at first sight?
- when did they start 'dating'?
- where and when did they first kiss?
- how long did they date?
- did they break up in the meantime?

Tip

Gather information
Depending on your relationship with the wedding couple, you might not know the answers to all of these questions. Have a chat with the couple's friends or family members, or go out for a pleasant dinner and gently question the bride and groom. If you want your book to be a surprise, of course you are not obliged to tell them why you are so curious!

You can choose to write your story with a text editing program or directly in the photo book as you compile it. If you are going to use a text editor, it is useful to make a note of the folder where you have stored the photos you want to use. If you include the file names or numbers right away, you will not need to look them up when you start compiling your photo book.

Like this, for example:

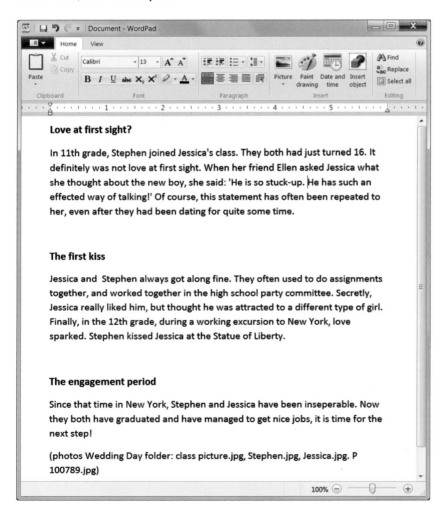

Love at first sight?

In 11th grade, Stephen joined Jessica's class. They both had just turned 16. It definitely was not love at first sight. When her friend Ellen asked Jessica what she thought about the new boy, she said: 'He is so stuck-up. He has such an effected way of talking!' Of course, this statement has often been repeated to her, even after they had been dating for quite some time.

The first kiss

Jessica and Stephen always got along fine. They often used to do assignments together, and worked together in the high school party committee. Secretly, Jessica really liked him, but thought he was attracted to a different type of girl. Finally, in the 12th grade, during a working excursion to New York, love sparked. Stephen kissed Jessica at the Statue of Liberty.

The engagement period

Since that time in New York, Stephen and Jessica have been inseperable. Now they both have graduated and have managed to get nice jobs, it is time for the next step!

(photos Wedding Day folder: class picture.jpg, Stephen.jpg, Jessica.jpg. P 100789.jpg)

☞ **Write a piece about the beginning of the couple's relationship**

The Proposal

There as many proposals as there are marriages, they will all be different. If the groom (or the bride) has proposed in a special or unusual way, you may want to include a story about the proposal in your book. Perhaps the groom proposed during half-time, in a match of his favorite football team or during a romantic holiday dinner. For example, you could write about:

- who asked whom?
- where did the whole thing happen?
- how did he or she propose?
- did she or he say yes immediately?

☞ **Write about the circumstances of the proposal**

If any pictures have been taken during or just after the event, you can also add these to the story.

☞ **Find a photo that refers to the marriage proposal**

The Wedding card

It is a great idea to add the couple's wedding card to your book. You can scan this card, just like a photo, and insert it into a photo box in your book.

 Tip

Scanning
In *Chapter 6 Collecting Photos* you can read all about scanning photos. You can scan other types of documents such as a wedding card in the same way.

☞ **Scan the front and back side of the wedding card**

You can always add extra text, if you have more information about the wedding card:
• who designed the card?
• is there some special story regarding the card?
• did the invitation come as a complete surprise or did everybody know beforehand that they were going to get married?

☞ **Write a story about the wedding card**

If you are going enter your text directly into your photo book, the page might look something like this:

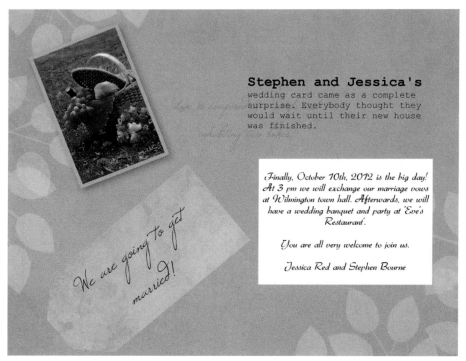

Stephen and Jessica's
wedding card came as a complete
surprise. Everybody thought they
would wait until their new house
was finished.

Finally, October 10th, 2012 is the big day!
At 3 pm we will exchange our marriage vows
at Wilmington town hall. Afterwards, we will
have a wedding banquet and party at 'Eve's
Restaurant'.

You are all very welcome to join us.

Jessica Red and Stephen Bourne

We are going to get married!

Program:
Mixbook

Theme Background

Font:
Courier New
Gabrielle
Windsong

The Preparations

Wedding preparations can be very elaborate. Choosing an appropriate setting for the wedding ceremony and the marriage feast is just one of the multitudes of things that have to be dealt with. Perhaps you were closely involved in these preparations and have some stories to tell.

For example:
- how many wedding locations were visited before the perfect location was finally found?
- why was this particular place chosen?
- did the couple have preliminary talks with the magistrate and/or priest or minister? Are there some interesting stories to tell about that?
- was it difficult to find a suitable location for the reception, the wedding banquet and the party? Did they try various dinner arrangements?

Perhaps you have some pictures of these preparations. For instance, photos of the couple visiting various locations or having dinner at one of the restaurants that was being considered for the wedding banquet.

The preparations

Jessica can smile again! They managed to find the perfect wedding location and a restaurant for the banquet and party, all on the same day. The location they had picked earlier, turned out to be fully booked on their wedding date, but today the received good news. They can get married in the beautiful Wilmington town hall!

This had to be celebrated, so they went out for dinner. By sheer luck, the ended up at a restaurant that also proved to be perfect for their wedding party! They did not hesitate a second and immediately booked the restaurant for their party!

Program:
Shutterfly

Standard background with embellishment

Effect B&W applied to all photos

Font:
Mrs Eaves

☞ **Write a story about the wedding preparations and find one or more matching photos**

The Wedding Dress

The Wedding Suit

An important part of the preparations is choosing the right dress for the bride and suit for the groom. Sometimes, the first dress in the bridal shop hits the mark, but usually it takes quite a while to find just the right attire for that special day.

You can simply include photos and descriptions of the wedding gown and suit in your book. But if you have more to tell about the search for suitable clothes, you can use as much space as you need to expand on your account. Here are some things to think about regarding the wedding attire:

- was it difficult to find the right dress, or were they successful at the first store?
- how many gowns did the bride try on (approximately)?
- who went along for the fitting?
- at which store did they finally buy the dress?
- why did they choose this particular dress?
- who accompanied the groom when he went shopping for a suit?
- did that go smoothly, or did it take longer?

☞ **Write a story about the wedding dress and wedding suit and find matching photos**

Program:
Blurb Booksmart

Theme Baroque

Font:
Khmer UI (title)
Garamond (text)

The Stag Nights and Bachelorette Parties

When young people get married, often a bachelor or bachelorette party will take place. The groom goes out for a night on the town with his brothers and friends, and the bride does exactly the same, accompanied by her sisters and girlfriends. There are lots of different ways for these parties to unfold. Sometimes, the bride or groom is dragged through town in an animal suit and he or she has to fulfill all kinds of crazy assignments. Sometimes the group engages in some kind of special activity, such as taking part in a workshop. But most of the time these parties will usually end up in a bar.

Anyhow, in the text you can describe what the party pictures are all about. These questions may help you expand your story further:
- who joined the bachelor party?
- which activities did they undertake?
- did anything special happen?
- where did the group have dinner?

☞ **Write a piece about the bachelor parties and find one or more matching photos**

Program: MyPublisher

Own photo as a background

Font: Segoe Print

The Bridesmaids and Groomsmen

If on this important day, the wedding couple is accompanied by a number of bridesmaids or flower girls, they deserve some attention too. The same goes for the groomsmen. You can create a separate page where they are portrayed.

Write about:
- who are the bridesmaids, flower girls, groomsmen, etcetera.
- what is their relationship with the happy couple

If you know of any funny anecdotes regarding the bridesmaids or groomsmen, don't be afraid to mention these in your story.

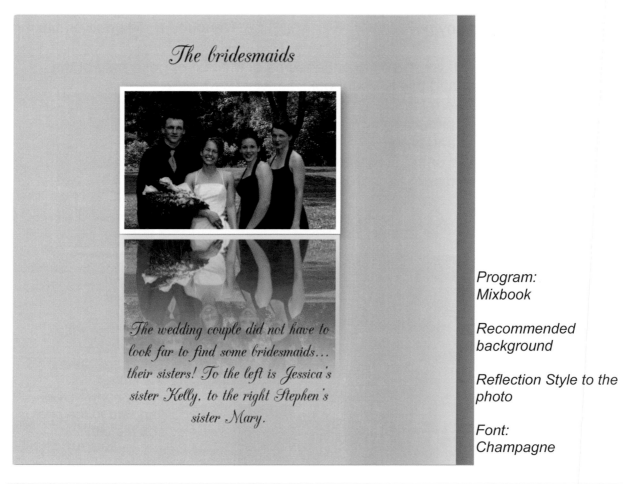

The bridesmaids

The wedding couple did not have to look far to find some bridesmaids... their sisters! To the left is Jessica's sister Kelly, to the right Stephen's sister Mary.

Program:
Mixbook

Recommended background

Reflection Style to the photo

Font:
Champagne

☞ **Write a story about the bridesmaids, groomsmen and other members of the wedding party and collect matching photos**

The Wedding Pictures

Most couples these days will hire a professional photographer to take their 'official' wedding pictures. If you are able to acquire some of these photos, you can add them to your book. You can also tell a bit more about the photo shoot:

- who took the pictures?
- where were the pictures taken?
- why did they choose this location?
- did anything special happen during the photo shoot?

☞ **Write a story about the wedding photos and collect matching photos**

A friend of Stephen's took the official wedding pictures in the park. Always convenient, to have a professional photographer in your circle of friends. Fortunately, the weather was beautiful and the results are great too.

Program:
MyPublisher

Own photo as a background, transparency 60%

Font: Tahoma

The Reception

The Gifts

No wedding day is without a reception. That is the moment when everyone gets the chance to congratulate the newlyweds and present them with gifts. In your wedding day story book you can use one or more pages to write about the reception.

For instance, write about:
- where the reception was held?
- how many guests were there?
- did anyone give a speech? what did he or she say?
- if you were present by the opening of the gifts, what types of things did the couple receive? Or, if they preferred receiving a contribution to some good cause: how much did the reception bring in?

After the photo shoot we all went to the reception at the restaurant 'The Jolly Joker' and had some nice food and drinks. The happy Barrett couple received lots of congratulations from more than 150 guests. Family and friends, colleagues: everybody was there.

In lieu of gifts, the couple had asked the guests to make a donation to the Born Free USA animal charity. The animals that are going to be saved by this charity can look forward to $ 3800, donated by the guests at the reception!

☞ **Write a story about the reception and collect matching photos**

The Wedding Cake

Be sure not to forget the wedding cake! Traditionally, the wedding couple has to cut the cake together. You will surely have some nice pictures of this occasion. Tell us about:

- what kind of cake did the couple choose?
- who baked the cake?
- did the decoration have any special meaning?

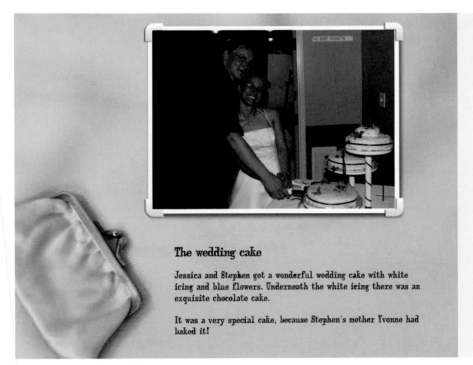

The wedding cake

Jessica and Stephen got a wonderful wedding cake with white icing and blue flowers. Underneath the white icing there was an exquisite chocolate cake.

It was a very special cake, because Stephen's mother Yvonne had baked it!

Program: Picaboo

Standard background photo

Corner applied around the photo

Font: Webster

☞ **Write a story about the wedding cake and find one or more matching photos**

The Wedding Banquet

The wedding banquet offers the couple and their guests a chance to catch their breath and relax a bit. This is the right time to enjoy a nice meal and review the day, but also to address the bride and groom. If you are going to write about the banquet, keep these topics in mind:

- how many guests were there?
- where was the banquet held?
- how did they lay out the tables, what was the table plan?
- what was the menu like?
- which persons held a speech, and what did they say?

By half past six in the evening the couple and twenty guests were seated for dinner at the restaurant 'The Jolly Joker'. They had laid a single, long table. The bride and groom were seated together at the head of the table.

For starters, the guests had a choice between beef Carpaccio or a prawn cocktail. After everyone had made his choice, it was time for the first speech. The father of the bride impressed it upon his son-in-law to take very good care of his daughter. Stephen promised to do this.

 Tip

Menu
If you can get hold of a wedding banquet menu, you can scan the menu and add it to your story.

☞ **Write a piece about the wedding banquet and the speeches and find one or more matching photos**

The Feast

The First Dance

The Entertainment

After dinner, the chairs can be put aside and it is time to party. You will probably be able to fill numerous pages with a description of the festivity. You can tell something about the band, songs played, when the bride and groom first danced together.

For instance, write about:
- where was the party held?
- what did the party hall look like? What was the layout, how was it decorated?
- how many guests were invited to the party?
- was there a band or a DJ?
- what kind of music did they play?
- did the couple start the dancing off with their favorite song?
- did anyone perform any special acts, or sing songs for the bride and groom? Who?
- did anything special occur during the party?

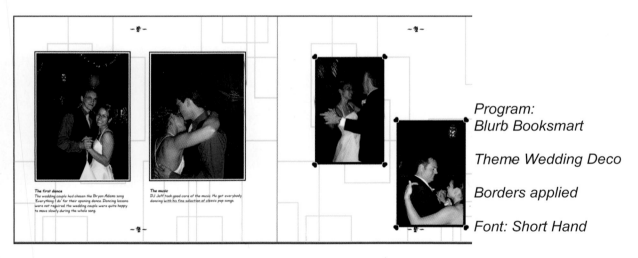

Program:
Blurb Booksmart

Theme Wedding Deco

Borders applied

Font: Short Hand

☞ **Write a story about the wedding party and the first dance and collect matching photos**

8.3 Your Own Photo Book

Hopefully, all the examples provided in this chapter have sufficiently inspired you to start writing your own story. You can elaborate as much as you want and make the wedding day story as long as you want:

- you can leave out the titles that do not apply to your story
- you can add extra titles for different activities, or special places and events

You can decide for yourself how much text you want to add to each topic. It may be enough just to add a caption to go along with all your photos. Don't be afraid to fill an entire page with text when you have something significant or interesting to tell about the wedding or the preparations for it. In this respect, the album software does not impose any restrictions.

 Tip

Read back
Take time once in a while to read over what you have written. You may decide to rephrase an item here and there or add extra lines to your story.

Finally, if you are satisfied with the contents of your book, you can send it to the print service and pay for it. In *Chapter 3 Working with Mixbook* you can read how to do this.

9. Tell Your Life Story

Do you have a child, grandchild, niece or nephew or even a friend that keeps asking you about the past? Do they want to know where you come from, where you went to school, and what things were like back in the "old days"? Or do they ask about the kind of jobs you've had, or where you met the love of your life? If you find yourself regularly answering these kinds of questions, you might consider creating a book.

This may not put an end to all of the questions, but by reading your story, people can get to know you a little better. More than likely, they will have more questions to ask. Your book can become quite handy at starting up a conversation with a family member or a friend.

In your book you can combine photos with your own story. You can elaborate as much as you want: short captions to go along with the photos, or a longer story that describes key events or a particular phase in your life. In this chapter we give you many ideas for writing an autobiographical story. You will also see various examples that have been made with the software from different providers.

In this chapter you can:

- read about an action plan that can be used to write an autobiographical story;
- read about the best way of structuring your story;
- get ideas for the contents and layout of your story, by looking at the examples.

 Please note!

The topics, titles and page headings used in this chapter are just meant to inspire you and give you some ideas. You do not have to use the exact same structure for your own book. Add or remove any topic, title or page heading that is better suited for your own story.

 Please note!

The length of your descriptive text can vary widely. In our examples we have restricted the length per topic to cover one or two pages. But, you can use more than two pages per topic if you desire. You can even fill an entire page with just text. It is entirely up to you.

Please note!

In each example shown in this chapter, we include the name of the photo book software it was made with as well as the formatting options used. Photo book software providers continue to improve their programs. It may occur that a particular background, template, frame or font is no longer available in the version of software you are using.

9.1 Action Plan

If you want to write a story about your life, you can follow a fixed action plan:

Step 1   Think about your story and write down some keywords that sum up what you want to tell.

Step 2   Collect the photos you want to use in your book and store them in a separate folder (see *Chapter 6 Collecting Photos*).

Step 3   Open the photo book software you are going to use, create a new project and select the desired format (see *Chapter 3 Working with Mixbook*).

Step 4   Create a cover for your book, if you wish (see *Chapter 3 Working with Mixbook*).

Step 5   Think about the type of image you want to project on your page and then select a suitable background in the photo book software (see *Chapter 3 Working with Mixbook*).

Step 6   Add text and photos to the page.

Step 7   Modify the layout: select a suitable format for the photo boxes and text boxes on the page. Select a font and font size for the text. If you want, you can also add frames, templates and clip art. (see *Chapter 3 Working with Mixbook*).

Repeat steps 5, 6, and 7 for all the pages in your book.

Step 8   Check all the pages, paying close attention to the formatting, headings and spelling (see *Chapter 4 Writing Tips* and *Chapter 5 Formatting Tips*).

Step 9   Send the album to the print service.

In the following section you will find more examples and some ideas for step 6.

 Tip

Short/long texts

If you are planning to write short pieces of text and want to use a lot of pictures, you can start using the photo book software right away.

If you want to write longer stories, it may be easier to write the full story in a text editing program first. Then later, you can insert the text into the photo book software. You can do this by copying and pasting the text into the book (see *Chapter 3 Working with Mixbook*).

9.2 The Structure of Your Story

If you are going to tell your life story, a chronological account would be the most logical option. You can start by telling something about your parents and your birth. You can interrupt the chronological flow now and then by writing something about a certain theme. For example, you might want to mention something about all the sports you have been involved with during your lifetime, or all the pets you have had.

You story can be as long or as short as you want. If writing comes easy to you, you can use longer pieces of text in your book, including descriptions and anecdotes. If you do not want to use lengthy texts, you can confine the text to simple captions accompanying each photo, describing the action or subject depicted and when it happened. You can construct your story using the topics, titles and headings in the following examples.

 Please note!

The topics, titles and page headings used in this chapter are just meant to inspire you and give you some ideas. You do not have to use the exact same structure for your own photo book. Add or remove a topic, title or page heading that is better suited for your own story.

My Parents

If you want to start from the beginning, you can include information about your parents. Your own children may still remember your parents, as they were their own grandparents, but your grandchildren will probably not know them or not very well. So it would be nice to know more about them, and see their picture.

For instance, you could write about:

- what are your parent's full names and when were they born?
- where do they come from?
- where did they meet?
- how old were they at that time?
- what kind of job did your father have? Did your mother work?
- when did they get married?

☞ **Write a story about your parents**

☞ **Find one or more matching photos**

You can choose to write your story with a text editing program or write directly in the photo book as you compile it. If you are going to use a text editor, it is useful to make a note of the folder where you have stored the photos you want to use. If you include the file names or numbers right away, you will not need to look them up when you start compiling your photo book.

Like this, for example:

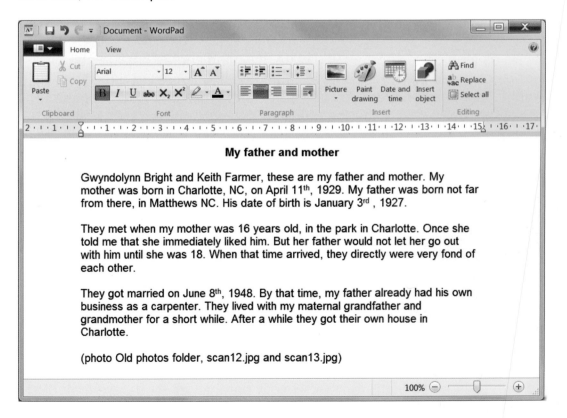

By entering the text directly into the photo book, your page may look something like this at the start:

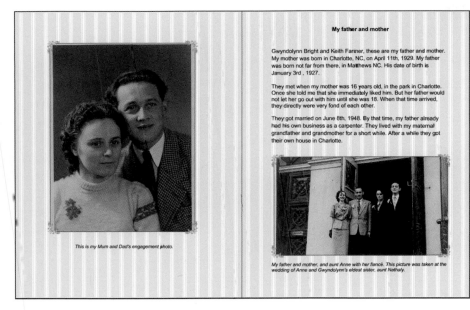

My father and mother

Gwyndolynn Bright and Keith Farmer, these are my father and mother. My mother was born in Charlotte, NC, on April 11th, 1929. My father was born not far from there, in Matthews NC. His date of birth is January 3rd , 1927.

They met when my mother was 16 years old, in the park in Charlotte. Once she told me that she immediately liked him. But her father would not let her go out with him until she was 18. When that time arrived, they directly were very fond of each other.

They got married on June 8th, 1948. By that time, my father already had his own business as a carpenter. They lived with my maternal grandfather and grandmother for a short while. After a while they got their own house in Charlotte.

This is my Mum and Dad's engagement photo.

My father and mother, and aunt Anne with her fiancé. This picture was taken at the wedding of Anne and Gwyndolynn's eldest sister, aunt Nathaly.

Program:
Blurb Booksmart

Standard background across two pages

Borders applied to the photos

Font: Arial

 Tip

View large examples
You can view larger examples of the pages in this book by visiting the website that accompanies the book: **www.visualsteps.com/photobook**

My Birth

Surely, somewhere you can muster up a photo of yourself as a baby. You can use this photo for the story about your birth. Write down everything you still know or have managed to find out, for example:
*   when and where were you born?
*   were you born at home or in the hospital?
*   where does your name come from, were you named after someone? Or does your name have any special significance?
*   where did your parents live at the time of your birth?
*   can you tell us anything special about your birth?

☞ **Write a story about the day you were born**

☞ **Find one or more matching photos**

Please note!

In the past, people did not take as many pictures as they do now. It does not matter if you do not have a photo of yourself as a newborn. You can also use a photo taken at a later date. It will still create a nice effect.

If you still have your birth announcement card, or a hospital birth record, it would be great to add these items to your book. You can scan these as if they were regular photos and insert them into a photo box.

 Tip

Scanning

In *Chapter 6 Collecting Photos* you can read all about scanning photos. You can scan other types of documents, such as a birth announcement, in the same way.

My birth

I was born on April 10th, 1949. At home, at my father's and mother's house on Apple street in Charlotte. My brothers and sisters were staying with our grandfather and grandmother. When they came home the discovered they had a new baby sister.

My parents claimed I hardly cried when I was a baby, and was very curious about everything going on around me. That has not changed a bit!

My parents called me Joanne Wynona Juliette. Wynona after my maternal grandmother, and Juliette after my father's mother. My parents simply liked the name 'Joanne' so that became my first name.

They have not helped me a lot, all those fancy names. I was the youngest and everyone has always called me Jo, right away. I was always glad if somebody asked me about my initials J.W.J. Then I could tell them about my beautiful names.

*Program:
Picaboo*

Theme Baby Blanket

Font: Hockey is Life

Brothers and Sisters

Do you have any brothers and sisters? You can include them in your book. If you answer the following questions, you will get some ideas of what you can write about:
- what are the full names of your brothers and sisters?
- when were they born?
- what is your place in the birth order?
- did they often have to take care of you when you were little?
- with whom (of your brothers and sisters) did you spend the most time?

☞ **Write a story about your brothers and sisters**

☞ **Find one or two matching photos**

It would be nice if you could find photos of your brothers and sisters when they were young and pair them with what they look like today.

 Tip

New photo
Do you have an old photo of you and your brothers and sisters? How about making a new photo of the same group the next time you meet? For example, during the holidays or at a reunion or a birthday party.

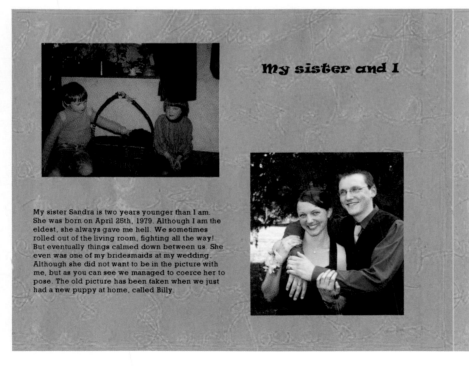

My sister and I

My sister Sandra is two years younger than I am. She was born on April 25th, 1979. Although I am the eldest, she always gave me hell. We sometimes rolled out of the living room, fighting all the way! But eventually things calmed down between us. She even was one of my bridesmaids at my wedding. Although she did not want to be in the picture with me, but as you can see we managed to coerce her to pose. The old picture has been taken when we just had a new puppy at home, called Billy.

Program:
MyPublisher

Collage Theme across two pages 50% transparency

Font:
Ravie (title)
Rockwell (text)

Kindergarten

Starting kindergarten is one of the first milestones in a child's life. You will surely have some stories to tell about that period. Maybe you do not clearly remember this time yourself, but your parents or brothers and sisters may have told you some stories. For example:

- how old were you when you first went to kindergarten?
- did you enjoy it, or not at all?
- which school did you go to?
- who was your teacher?
- can you still remember your first day at school, or, in general, your school days?
- did you go home for lunch, or stay over at school?
- who was your best friend in kindergarten?
- what did you like to do best in kindergarten?
- did you get a report card in kindergarten? If you still have it, what does it say?
- do you remember any funny anecdotes from those days?

☞ **Write a story about your kindergarten days**

Do you have an old picture of your school, or an old class photo or a portrait made by the school photographer? If not, you can use other photos of yourself as a small child. Does your kindergarten school still exist? Then you can take a new picture of the building too.

☞ **Find one or more matching photos**

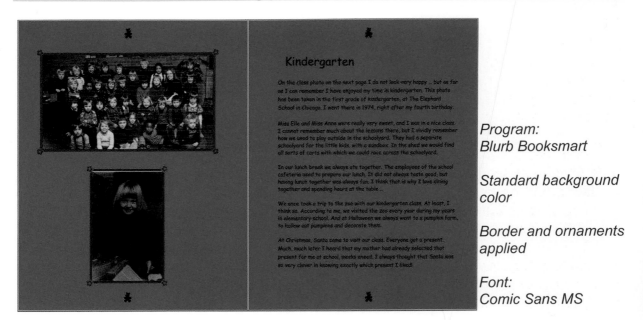

Program:
Blurb Booksmart

Standard background
color

Border and ornaments
applied

Font:
Comic Sans MS

Memories of Your Youth

You can use this general title to include all of the memories of your early childhood. These can be very diverse, for instance:

- what sort of toys did you have?
- what was your favorite toy?
- which games did you play outside? And with whom?
- did you have to help out at home? What were your chores? What did you think of this?
- what kind of a boy or girl were you? A ringleader, or rather shy and quiet?
- did you ever stay the night at a friend's house?
- did you go on family vacations in those years? Where did you go?
- did you ever get in trouble? What were you up to?

☞ Write a story about your childhood

It is likely that you will remember all sorts of things while browsing through old photo albums. You can scan these old photos and use them to illustrate your story.

☞ Find one or more matching photos

You can spread your childhood memories over multiple pages. A page on staying overnight at a friend's house, a page on the chores at home, a page on the games you played, etc. Like this, for example:

Marbles

As a child I used to love playing the game of marbles. Together with the boy next door, Peter, I used to play marbles for hours, in the park. We took turns tossing two or three marbles. Then we tried to shove the marbles into the hole. If you succeeded, you could try again with a new marble. But if you missed, it was the other one's turn.

The goal was to be the one to get the last marble into the hole. The winner would be able to keep all the marbles! We both had a big fat bag of marbles, but we still wanted more, especially those extra large, beautiful marbles. I must confess that I had to cry sometimes, when I lost some of these marbles to my friend Peter. But he was such a sweet guy; he often let me win them all back!

But playing marbles did leave its marks. After a summer full of playing marbles, I could not get the dirt off my index finger! The dirt off the street had ingrained itself in my finger from the continuous shoving through the mud or over the pavement.

Elementary School

After kindergarten came elementary school. At the age of six you usually start to learn how to read and write. Do you remember something about these times? Was your elementary school in the same familiar building as your kindergarten class? Or did you have to go a new school? By answering these and the following questions you may get some ideas to write something about:

- in which year did you go to elementary school?
- which school did you attend?
- what kind of a pupil were you? Industrious, or lazy?
- was studying easy for you?
- who were your favorite teachers at elementary school? Why?
- did you get along with your teachers? If not, why?
- which subjects did you enjoy, and which not?
- did you repeat a class in elementary school, or maybe even skip a class?
- did you go home for your lunch, or did you stay over?
- did you sit next to someone, and who was this?
- who were your best friends at the time?
- did you ever go on a field trip or an excursion during elementary school? Where to? How did you like it?

☞ **Write a story about your elementary school days**

If you have kept any photos from the school photographer, you can use one or more of these in your photo book. Or use other photos from that period. Does your elementary school still exist? You may want to take a new picture of the building.

☞ **Find one or more matching photos**

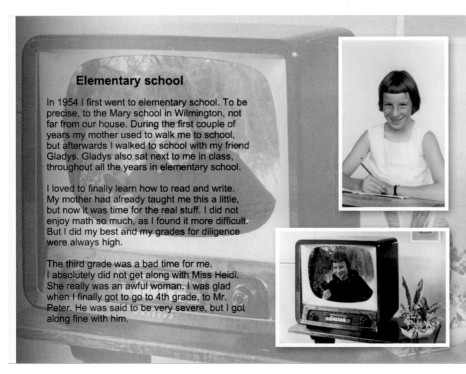

Elementary school

In 1954 I first went to elementary school. To be precise, to the Mary school in Wilmington, not far from our house. During the first couple of years my mother used to walk me to school, but afterwards I walked to school with my friend Gladys. Gladys also sat next to me in class, throughout all the years in elementary school.

I loved to finally learn how to read and write. My mother had already taught me this a little, but now it was time for the real stuff. I did not enjoy math so much, as I found it more difficult. But I did my best and my grades for diligence were always high.

The third grade was a bad time for me. I absolutely did not get along with Miss Heidi. She really was an awful woman. I was glad when I finally got to go to 4th grade, to Mr. Peter. He was said to be very severe, but I got along fine with him.

Program: Mixbook

Own photo as a background, 51% transparency

Black and white effect applied to the photos

Font: Arial

My Teens

You can use this title to combine the memories you have from when you were a teenager. If you still remember lots of things from this period, do not hesitate to use multiple pages for this topic. Here are some suggestions for things you could write about:

- were you a difficult youngster or were you easy-going? How did this manifest itself?
- did you belong to a specific group?
- what was your favorite music?
- which books did you like to read?
- what were your favorite TV shows?
- did you go to the movies once in a while? What were your favorite movies?
- who was your favorite movie star?
- what did your room look like? Which posters did you hang on your walls, for example?
- did you have a job? What did you do, and how much did you earn?
- did you go out sometimes? Where, and with whom?
- did you participate in any sports? What kind of sports? Were you on a team?
- who was your best friend?
- did you go on vacation during your teenage years? Where, how, and with whom?

☞ **Write a story about your teens**

By looking at the photos from this period of your life, you are bound to remember many other things. You can use these photos to illustrate this part of your story. You can spread the memories of your teenage years across several pages. A page on the sports you participated in, a page about the job you had, or one about your special interests, a favorite musician, a movie or television star. Like this, for example:

Music music music

While digging in the heaps of old photos I suddenly notice that in a lot of pictures, I am wearing a headphone. In the top photo I am 13 years old. Sitting in a bean bag chair next to the record player, I am wearing a big headphone and listening to the records in my parents' collection. Even then, I loved Queen, Bob Dylan, and Crosby, Stills & Nash.

Meanwhile I often read a book, or Donald Duck comics. But usually I read the song texts printed on the record sleeve.

The photo at the bottom was taken two years later. In the mean time I had acquired a walkman, and a slightly smaller headphone. I even used to record tapes of radio broadcasts, or tape the records of my big hero Bruce Springsteen. In 1984 his epic record 'Born in the USA' came out. I was completely hooked. And it never went away. By the way, I also still read Donald Duck comics, once in a while.

Program:
MyPublisher

No background

Font:
Malgun Gothic

☞ **Find one or more matching photos**

Middle School/ Junior High / High School

You can describe your middle school/high school days in the same way as your elementary school days. For instance, use these questions as a guide for your story:
- in which year did you first go to middle school or high school?
- what was the name of the school? where was it located?
- what type of school was it? For example, public or private, junior high, middle school, high school, vocational training, etcetera.
- what kind of student were you? Did you get high grades without too much effort, or did you have to work hard for some subjects?
- which were your favorite subjects?
- which subjects or classes did you hate? Why?
- did you ever have to repeat a class, or did you skip a class perhaps?

- did you have lots of homework? Did you finish your homework on your own? Or did someone have to remind you about it?
- who were your favorite teachers? Why?
- which teachers didn't you like? Why?
- did you participate in extracurricular activities? For example, were you a member of the school drama club, debating team, the student government, or did you write articles for the school newspaper?
- how did you get to school? By bicycle, on foot, or by car or bus?
- did you sit next to someone you liked?
- who were your best friends at the time?
- did you go on any field trips, study trips or other excursions? Where to? How did you like it?
- do you remember something about a school dance, a football game or another special event?

☞ **Write a story about your middle school, junior high or high school days**

☞ **Find one or more matching photos**

Going to Mendocino High School

In 1982 my junior high school days were over. I used to walk to school, but Mendocino High was much further and I had to use the school bus to get to this much bigger school. The trip took about a half an hour, one-way.

The 9th graders had their own separate building, called 'The Bridge'. This was fine, because it made the transition from my tiny junior high to the big high school across town much easier. It was still quite a change. Different teachers, different classes, more rules, and lots of homework…

Eventually I got the hang of it and started to like high school. I was a good enough student, which meant that I had time for other activities. The student council, the school newspaper, the community service project, the softball team… I really loved it all! I remember when we had to organize a special activity for our community service project, at that time a charity in Brazil. We got to bake pancakes in the mornings and we were actually allowed to miss some of our classes to do this. We sold the pancakes during the lunch breaks. We were so proud of the money we managed to raise.

My first friend

Do you still remember your first boyfriend's or girlfriend's name? Most people have a very clear memory of their first serious love affair. It deserves some attention in your story.

For instance, write about this:
- what was the name of your friend?
- where did you meet him or her?
- how old were you at that time, and how old was he or she?
- how did you finally start 'going out' together?
- how long did you date?
- when did you break up?

☞ **Write a story about your first love**

☞ **Find one or more matching photos**

My first girlfriend

On this old, torn picture you can see me with the girl next door, Janine. She was my first girlfriend. At least... I had decided that she was to be my girlfriend. She knew nothing about it and I did not dare to tell her this. You see, I was only eight years old, and she was eleven. And she was 8 inches taller than me. She liked to play outside with the little boy next door, but that was all. But oh boy, was I madly in love!

Program: Shutterfly

Style Pretty Pink

Sticker applied

Font: Neutraface Book

College/University

If you went to college or university after you finished high school, you will probably have lots of things to write about:
- when did you go to college?
- which college or university did you attend?
- which subject(s) did you study? Why did you choose those subjects?
- where did you live during your college days? Did you live alone, or on campus?
- were you a member of a sorority or fraternity? If so, which one? What kind of activities did they organize?
- did your studies go well, or were you too busy enjoying life as a student?
- did you participate in sports? Were you on the college team?
- where did you go out in those days?
- who were your best friends at the time?
- did you do any internships or traineeships during your studies? Where and with which company?
- did you go abroad for a semester?
- did you write a final thesis? On which subject?
- did you graduate, eventually? Which diploma or degree did you obtain?

☞ **Write a story about your college/university days and find one or more matching photos**

 Please note!

If you did not go to college or university, you can skip this topic, of course.

True Love

Finally, a day arrives… when you meet your true love. Sometimes, Cupid's arrow strikes very early on. The first high school friend turns out to be your one true love. Others might meet Mr. or Mrs. Right when they go to college, or even much later on. How was it for you:
- who is your big love?
- where did you meet him or her?
- how old were you at that time?
- was it love at first sight? Or did it take years of friendship to ignite the fire?
- how did you start dating him or her? Any nice anecdotes to go with it?
- when did you first kiss?
- how long did you date?
- did you ever break up for a short while, during this time?
- who proposed to whom? Where? How did it go?
- how long were you engaged?

☞ **Write a story about your one true love and find one or more matching photos**

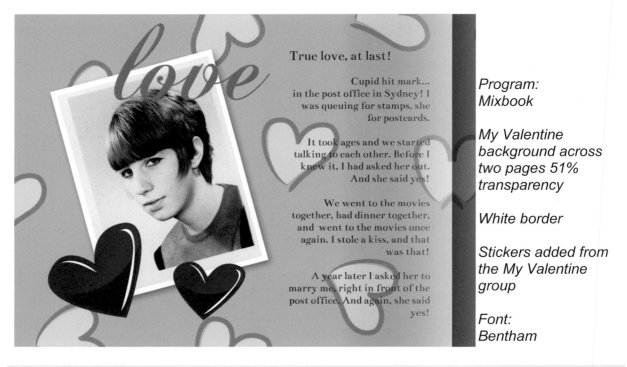

True love, at last!

Cupid hit mark... in the post office in Sydney! I was queuing for stamps, she for postcards.

It took ages and we started talking to each other. Before I knew it, I had asked her out. And she said yes!

We went to the movies together, had dinner together, and went to the movies once again. I stole a kiss, and that was that!

A year later I asked her to marry me, right in front of the post office. And again, she said yes!

Program: Mixbook

My Valentine background across two pages 51% transparency

White border

Stickers added from the My Valentine group

Font: Bentham

Our Wedding Day

If you married your true love, be sure to add the story of your wedding day to your book. You can expand the story as much as you like. Here are just a few of the many things you could share:

- when did you get married?
- where did you get married?
- what kind of dress did the bride wear?
- what kind of suit did the groom wear?
- who were the witnesses?
- were there any bridesmaids/groomsmen or flower children?
- who attended the ceremony?
- did you only marry in front of a civil servant, or in church as well?
- do you still remember anything from the speeches at the town hall or in church?
- how did the day pass? Did anything funny, crazy, or special happen?
- did you have a wedding cake? What did it look like?
- did you have a wedding banquet or a feast that day? Who were the guests?
- did you dance to your favorite song?
- were there any remarkable speeches, songs, or performers?
- what was the most special wedding gift?
- did you go on a honeymoon? Where?

☞ **Write a story about your wedding day**

☞ **Find one or more matching photos**

Program: Shutterfly | Theme Watercolor Wedding | Font: Fling

 Tip

More ideas and examples

In *Chapter 8 Create a Wedding Day Book* you will find many more ideas and examples.

All the Places I Have Lived In

If you are someone that has had to move many times, it may be nice to show a summary of all the places you have lived in. Here are some things you could write about:

- how many times did you move in your life?
- where did you live, and for how long?
- what were the reasons for moving?

The summation could look something like this:

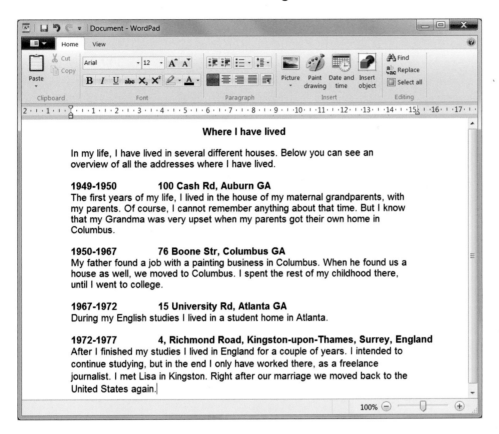

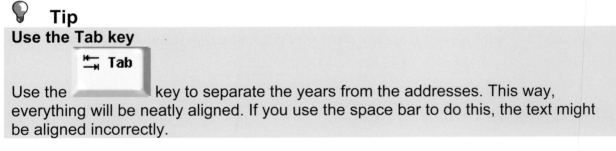

Tip

Use the Tab key

Use the ⭾ Tab key to separate the years from the addresses. This way, everything will be neatly aligned. If you use the space bar to do this, the text might be aligned incorrectly.

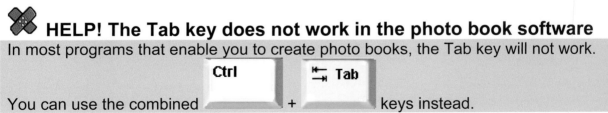

HELP! The Tab key does not work in the photo book software

In most programs that enable you to create photo books, the Tab key will not work.

You can use the combined **Ctrl** + **⭾ Tab** keys instead.

If you have any photos from the various places you have lived in, you can add them to your story album.

☞ **Write a story about your different places of residence and find one or more matching photos**

My Career

Did you get your first job right after finishing high school (or college)? If you have worked for several different companies since then, you can present a short summary of employment on a single page. For instance, like this:

1970 - 1972	*Johnson Printing Office*	*apprentice*
1972 - 1975	*Johnson Printing Office*	*typesetter*
1975 - 1980	*Frank's Printing Business*	*printer/tutor*
1980 - 1985	*Frank's Printing Business*	*offset printer*
etcetera.		

In the pages that follow, you can tell a bit more about the companies and your jobs:
- what was the first job you ever applied for? How did it go? Did they accept you?
- what was your first job?
- at which company? Can you tell us a bit more about that company?
- what kind of job did you have?
- did you like it?
- how long did you have that job?
- did you receive a promotion with the company, or did they give you a better job?

The story of your various jobs does not necessarily have to be a tedious, boring list. You could include these topics:
- who were your favorite colleagues?
- did you have other tasks within the company, besides your regular job, for example, member of the personnel committee or union representative?
- did you witness any company milestones, for instance, a company anniversary or the introduction of a new product?
- at which company did you celebrate an anniversary yourself?

My career started at Billy's Candy. I worked there for nine years. First in Sales, then as a salesman on the travelling sales force. During my employment I also took a course in marketing.

My career took a giant step forward when I changed jobs. I got a job at Walmart, as an account manager. First in the candy department, where I helped develop Asterix and Obelix candies. Afterwards I also worked in the coffee and wine departments.

I always enjoyed working, at Billy's Candy as well as at Walmart. Both companies offered me the opportunity to learn and develop my career.

After work, lots of activities were organized. At Billy's Candy we used to play a lot of American football. On the photo in the centre I am awarded the second prize in the tournament, on behalf of the sales department.

With Obelix, and in the background you see a display with sweets.

Second prize American football tournament.

With a colleague, in the wine department of a supermarket.

Program:
My Publisher

Standard background color Gray

Font: Tahoma

☞ **Write a story about your career and collect matching photos**

Our Children

- what was it like to become a father or mother for the first time?
- when were your children born?
- what are their full names, birth dates and places of birth?
- are there any special stories to tell about their birth?
- how did you come by their names? Were they named after someone or do the names have any special meaning?
- how were your children when they were babies/toddlers/infants, etcetera.
- did they get along with each other?
- did they go to daycare when they were little? Why or why not?
- where did they go to kindergarten and elementary school? How did this go?

💡 **Tip**

Expand your story
You can elaborate as much as you want, while telling stories about your children. For example, do you want to write a longer story about your son's or daughter's teenage years? Then you can use the questions from the *My Teens* topic to help you compose your story.

☞ **Write a story about your children**

☞ Find one or more matching photos

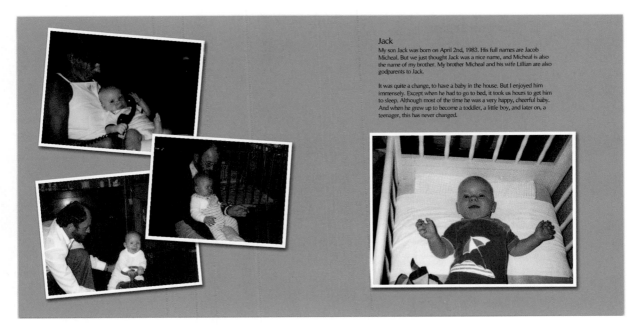

Jack

My son Jack was born on April 2nd, 1983. His full names are Jacob Micheal. But we just thought Jack was a nice name, and Micheal is also the name of my brother. My brother Micheal and his wife Lillian are also godparents to Jack.

It was quite a change, to have a baby in the house. But I enjoyed him immensely. Except when he had to go to bed, it took us hours to get him to sleep. Although most of the time he was a very happy, cheerful baby. And when he grew up to become a toddler, a little boy, and later on, a teenager, this has never changed.

Program: Picaboo | Standard background color | Border applied to the photos | Font: RomanSerif

Our Sons and Daughters-in-Law

Eventually children grow up. They meet their own Mr. or Mrs. Right and your family expands. You now have a son or daughter-in-law. Find some suitable pictures and describe the following things, for example:

- what are their names?
- who belongs to whom?
- when did they first visit your home?
- did your children date a lot before finding their true love?
- did they go out for a long time?
- are there any funny or embarrassing stories from this period?
- when did your children get married?

A NEW SON IN LAW

In January 2000 Emma brought Arnold to our house for the first time, and right away we could tell that he was here to stay. His predecessors have never ever been introduced to us. So when he was introduced, we knew enough! They got married on November 15th, 2005.

Program:
Shutterfly

Style Fresh and Fun

☞ **Write a piece about your son or daughter-in-law and collect matching photos**

Our Grandchildren

- when were your grandchildren born?
- what are their names? Were they named after you, by chance?
- who do they look like?
- do you babysit a lot? Which games do you play, or where do you take them?

☞ **Write a story about your grandchildren**

☞ **Find one or more matching photos**

 Tip

Expand your story
You can write as much as you want about your grandchildren. For instance, give each grandchild his or her own special double page. After that you can add some pages for the things you do together with all of your grandchildren.

Program:
Mixbook

Theme Baby Girl

Applied stickers

Font: Pixie

Pets

For many people, pets are an important part of their daily lives. If this is true for you, why not include an overview of all the pets you have had in your story. For instance, write about:

- which pets did you have in your youth?
- do you still remember their names?
- do you know any funny stories about the pets in your family?

Program:
Shutterfly

Theme Zoo Animals

Applied stickers and Leaf Medium Line frames

Font: Modern Wide

☞ **Write a story about your pets and find one or more matching photos**

Traveling

If you like to travel, you may want to include some of your travel stories in your book. If you make a list of all the trips you have made, and it is rather long, it will soon be boring. It is much better to describe the highlights of the various journeys you have made. Here are some things to think about:

- how did your parents travel when you were a child? Hiking, by car, did you go abroad? Did you travel by boat or by airplane?
- where did you go on your first journey abroad?
- your first vacation without your parents: what did you do? For example, did you hitchhike, or travel by train with a group of friends?
- did you go on a honeymoon? Where to? Why did you choose that specific location?
- how did you spend your holidays when you were in a steady relationship?
- did the holidays change once you had kids?
- have you ever taken a trip with your grandchildren?

It is easy to fill an entire page with a single, memorable trip:

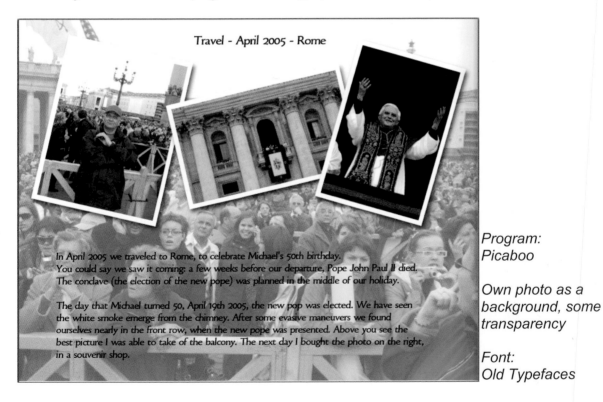

Travel - April 2005 - Rome

In April 2005 we traveled to Rome, to celebrate Michael's 50th birthday.
You could say we saw it coming: a few weeks before our departure, Pope John Paul II died.
The conclave (the election of the new pope) was planned in the middle of our holiday.

The day that Michael turned 50, April 19th 2005, the new pop was elected. We have seen the white smoke emerge from the chimney. After some evasive maneuvers we found ourselves nearly in the front row, when the new pope was presented. Above you see the best picture I was able to take of the balcony. The next day I bought the photo on the right, in a souvenir shop.

Program:
Picaboo

Own photo as a background, some transparency

Font:
Old Typefaces

Tip

More ideas and examples
In *Chapter 7 Create a Vacation Photo Book* you will find many more ideas and examples.

☞ **Write a story about all your travels and collect matching photos**

My Hobbies

Sports

Another great theme for your book is a story about the hobbies you have acquired. For many people, participating in a particular sport is their biggest hobby. If this also applies to you, you could write about:
- in what sports or physical activities have you participated during your lifetime?
- which clubs did you belong to?
- what was your favorite sport?
- what level did you reach with this sport or physical activity?
- how much time did you spend participating in this sport?
- which milestones (championships, for example) did you achieve in this sport?

Maybe you have quite a different hobby instead of a sport, such as collecting old postcards or records, needlework, some craft, woodworking, drawing or reading. Then you can write about the following things:
- which hobbies did you have?
- did your hobbies change throughout the years? Why?
- did you join a club for a specific hobby (for example, collecting stamps)?
- how much time did you spend on your hobbies, during various periods in your life?

☞ **Write a story about your sport or other hobbies and collect matching photos**

9.3 Your Own Story

Hopefully, the examples in this chapter have provided enough inspiration for you to write your own story. You can make your own autobiographical story as long and as expansive as you want:

- you can leave out the topics that do not apply to your own story, and
- you can add extra topics for other phases or key events in your life.

It is up to you how much text you add to each page. You can confine yourself to writing simple captions that go with the photos, or you can fill an entire page with text. In this respect, the album software does not impose any restrictions.

 Tip

Read back
Take time once in a while to read over what you have written. You may decide to rephrase an item here and there or add extra lines to your story.

 Tip

Describe a specific period
The structure we have used in this chapter is also useful if you just want to write about a certain period, phase or a key event in your life. For instance: *My Adventures in the UK*. You can choose various titles and page headings to go along with this topic, describing in detail the things that happened or the activities you were involved in.

Finally, if you are satisfied with the contents of your book, you can send it to the print service and pay for it. In *Chapter 3 Working with Mixbook* you can read how to do this.

10. Write About Baby's First Year

Can you think of another event that induces people to take more pictures than that of the birth of a new baby! Especially since nearly everyone these days owns a digital camera. In times past, people did not take so many pictures. The photos that were available were carefully pasted in a baby album. The album was also used to write about the development of the baby. Milestones such as when the baby laughed for the first time, when the baby first sat up, first started to crawl or when the first tooth appeared could be described in the album.

Do you have a new baby in your own family? You can use photo book software to compile a baby book yourself. You can write a story about the first year of the baby, perhaps your own grandchild, and combine the prettiest photos from your collection with your own story. You can expand as much as you want: short captions to go with the photos, or a more elaborate story of all your fond memories. In this way, you can create a book that is much more extensive than the traditional baby book.

In this chapter we will present many ideas for a baby book. You will find a number of examples of baby book pages which have been created with the software from different providers.

In this chapter you can:

- read about an action plan for creating a story about the first year of a baby's life;
- read about the best way of structuring your story;
- get ideas for the contents and layout of your story, by looking at the examples.

 Please note!

This chapter offers several examples of titles that you can use for your story. But of course you are not obliged to use all of these titles. You can skip some of them, rename them and add your own titles or headings as you go.

 Please note!

The length of your descriptive text can vary widely.
In our examples we have restricted the length per topic to cover one or two pages. But, you can use more than two pages per topic if you desire. You can even fill an entire page with just text. It is entirely up to you.

➷ Please note!

In each example shown in this chapter, we include the name of the photo book software it was made with as well as the formatting options used. Photo book software providers continue to improve their programs. It may occur that a particular background, template, frame or font is no longer available in the version of software you are using.

10.1 Action Plan

If you want to write a story about a baby's first or any other type of story, for that matter, you can follow a fixed action plan:

Step 1   Think about your story and write down some keywords that sum up what you want to tell.

Step 2   Collect the photos you want to use in your book and store them in a separate folder (see *Chapter 6 Collecting Photos*).

Step 3   Open the photo book software you are going to use, create a new project and select the desired format (see *Chapter 3 Working with Mixbook*).

Step 4   Create a cover for your book, if you wish (see *Chapter 3 Working with Mixbook*).

Step 5   Think about the type of image you want to project on your page and then select a suitable background in the photo book software (see *Chapter 3 Working with Mixbook*).

Step 6   Add text and photos to the page.

Step 7   Modify the layout: select a suitable format for the photo boxes and text boxes on the page. Select a font and font size for the text. If you want, you can also add frames, templates and clip art. (see *Chapter 3 Working with Mixbook*).

Repeat steps 5, 6, and 7 for all the pages in your book.

Step 8   Check all the pages, paying close attention to the formatting, headings and spelling (see *Chapter 4 Writing Tips* and *Chapter 5 Formatting Tips*).

Step 9   Send the album to the print service.

In the following section you will find more examples and some ideas for step 6.

Tip

Short/long texts
If you are planning to write short pieces of text and want to use a lot of pictures, you can start using the photo book software right away.
If you want to write longer stories, it may be easier to write the full story in a text editing program first. Then later, you can insert the text into the photo book software. You can do this by copying and pasting the text into the book (see *Chapter 3 Working with Mixbook*).

10.2 The Structure of Your Baby Book

If you are going to tell the story of a baby's first year, a chronological account would be the most logical option. For example, you can start by writing about the baby's parents and the day the baby was born. You can document the baby's development throughout the year, concluding your story with the celebration of the first birthday. Once in a while, you can insert stories about a specific theme in the chronological account, for instance, a favorite cuddly toy, first solid food, or the time you first performed babysitting duties!

Your story can be as long or as short as you want. If writing comes easy to you, you can use longer pieces of text in your book, including descriptions and anecdotes. If you do not want to use lengthy texts, you can confine the text to simple captions accompanying each photo, describing the action or subject depicted and when it happened. You can construct your story using the topics, titles and headings from the following examples.

Please note!

The topics, titles and page headings used in this chapter are just meant to inspire you and give you some ideas. You do not have to use the exact same structure for your own photo book. Add or remove any topic, title or page heading that is better suited for your own story.

Tip

For whom?
Before you start writing, think about the public for whom the book is intended. Do you want to address the baby, the parents or a wider audience? By writing about the baby in the third person singular ("He got his first tooth…") you create distance. By directly speaking to the child ("You got your first tooth …"), your story will become more intimate.

Mom and Dad

The best way to start a story about a baby's first year is by relaying some information about the parents. For instance, you can write about:
- the names of the parents
- where do they come from?
- where did they meet?
- how old were they at the time?
- did they get married? If so, when?

☞ Write a story about the parents

☞ Find one or more matching photos

You can choose to write your story with a text editing program or write directly in the photo book as you compile it. If you are going to use a text editor, it is useful to make a note of the folder where you have stored the photos you want to use. If you include the file names or numbers right away, you will not need to look them up when you start compiling your photo book.

Like this, for example:

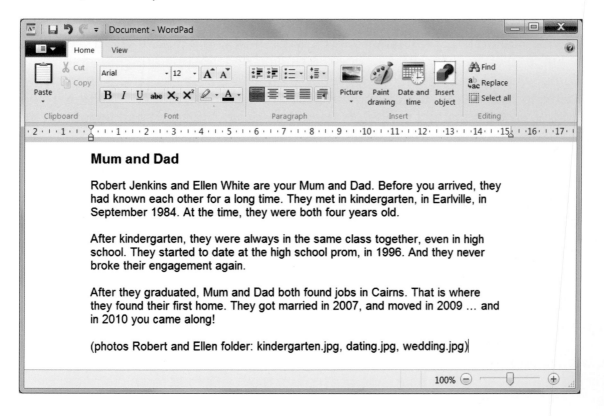

The preparations

Your baby room is ready for use

Before the new baby arrives, lots of things need to be done. The baby's room needs to be decorated and painted and furniture needs to be acquired. You can write about these preparations. For instance, describe the following things:

- how were the colors for the nursery chosen?
- who helped to paint and decorate the room?
- was it easy to find the right furniture, or did it take a long time?
- is there something special to say about the cradle or crib? Is it a family heirloom, for example? Who made the bedding?
- do any other pieces of furniture in the baby's room have a special story?

☞ **Write a story about the baby's room**

☞ **Find one or more matching photos**

If you enter your text directly into your photo book, the page might look something like this:

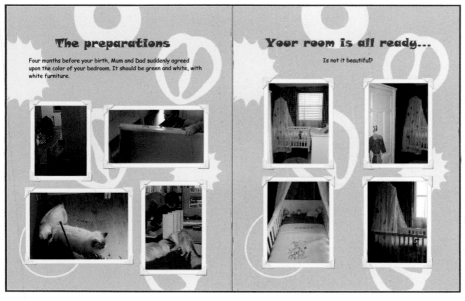

Program:
Blurb Booksmart

Standard background across two pages

Borders applied to the photos

Font:
Snap ITC (title)
Comic Sans MS (text)

Your Birth

How Did You Come By Your Name?

Do you have any photos of the first minutes after the baby was born? Then you can use these to fill the pages that describe the birth. You could tell something about:

- when and where the baby was born
- was that at home or in the hospital?
- where does the baby's name come from? Is the baby named after someone? Or does the name have some other special meaning?
- are there any special stories to tell about the birth?

☞ **Write a story about the birth and the baby's name**

☞ **Find one or more matching photos**

➥ **Please note!**

If you do not have any photos of the first moments of a baby's life, that does not matter. A picture that was taken a little later on will also create a nice effect.

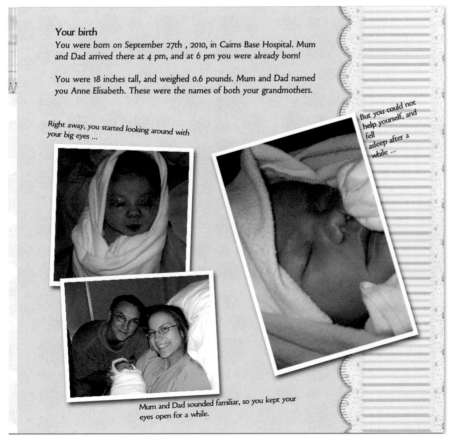

Your birth
You were born on September 27th , 2010, in Cairns Base Hospital. Mum and Dad arrived there at 4 pm, and at 6 pm you were already born!

You were 18 inches tall, and weighed 0.6 pounds. Mum and Dad named you Anne Elisabeth. These were the names of both your grandmothers.

Right away, you started looking around with your big eyes ...

But you could not help yourself, and fell asleep after a while ...

Mum and Dad sounded familiar, so you kept your eyes open for a while.

Program: Picaboo

Style Little Sweetheart

Font: Old Typefaces

The Birth Announcement

It is also nice to add a photo of the birth announcement to your photo book. You can scan this card as if it were a photo and insert it into a photo box.

 Tip

Scanning

In *Chapter 6 Collecting Photos* you can read how to scan photos. You can also scan other types of documents, such as a birth announcement, in the same way as you scan photos.

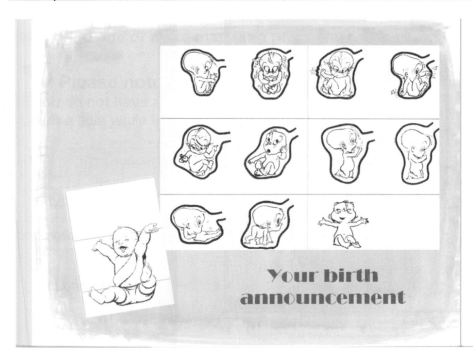

Program: MyPublisher

Oh baby boy theme background

Font: Broadway

☞ **Scan the birth announcement**

If you can think of a special story about this birth announcement, you can add some extra text. For instance:
- why was this particular card or text chosen? Or:
- who designed the card?

☞ **Write a story about the birth announcement**

Roll Over!

When a baby is about four or five months old, he or she will be able to roll over on his or her side. A few weeks later, the baby will even be able to roll from its back on to its belly, or vice versa. Some babies start rolling over when they are just three months old, but others only learn to master the trick when they are six months old. Whatever the case, once the baby is lying on the couch or on the bed and knows how to roll over, that's when the parents need to start worrying! You can write about these moments:

- when did the baby roll over on its side for the first time?
- when did the baby roll over on its belly? Where was he or she lying at the time?
- who were present?
- did the baby ever nearly roll off the couch or bed?

 Write a story about rolling over

 Find one or more matching photos

➥ **Please note!**

If you do not have a photo of the baby rolling over, you can skip this topic. But you can also decide to just write a few lines about baby's rolling abilities.

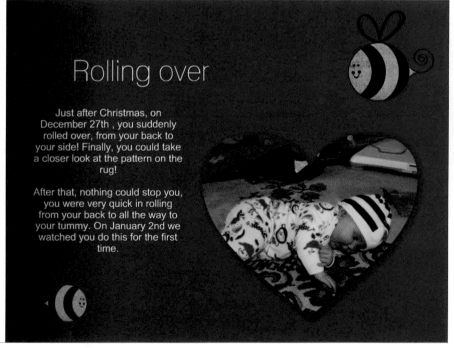

Program:
Mixbook

Standard background color

Shape style applied to photo

Stickers added

Font:
Lane Narrow (title)
Arial (text)

The First Taste of Fruit

The First Taste of Vegetables

The First…

After a few months, the baby does not just need milk, but starts to eat its first meals of solid food, such as fruit and vegetables. Naturally, each child will react in a different way to this new food. For instance, write about:

- when did the baby eat his or her first bite of fruit?
- what kind of fruit was it? Homemade or from the store?
- how did it go? Did he or she like it, or not at all?
- which was the favorite fruit?
- when did the baby eat vegetables for the first time?
- what kind of vegetables? Homemade or from the store?
- how did it go? Did he or she like it, or not at all?
- which were the favorite vegetables?
- is there any other 'first food' about which you can tell a nice story?

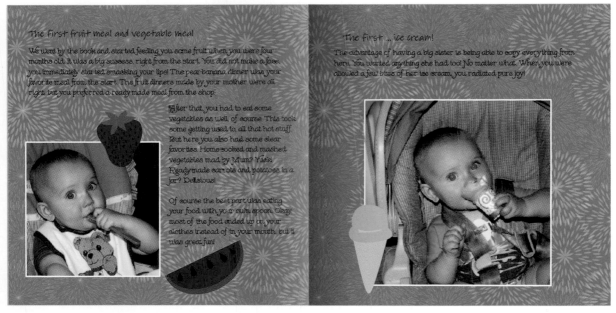

Program: Shutterfly | Theme Summer Splash | Stickers added | Font: Lindsey (title) Gasoline Alley (text)

Sitting!

Once the baby has learned how to roll over, it is time to learn how to sit. With a little bit of support behind the back, most babies are able to sit up when they are between three and six months old. Between six and nine months they will start to be much steadier, and when they reach nine months they usually know how to sit up without any help. You can document the baby's stages of learning how to sit in your book. For instance, write about:

- when was the baby able to sit up without support?
- when did he or she sit up by himself or herself?
- who were present?

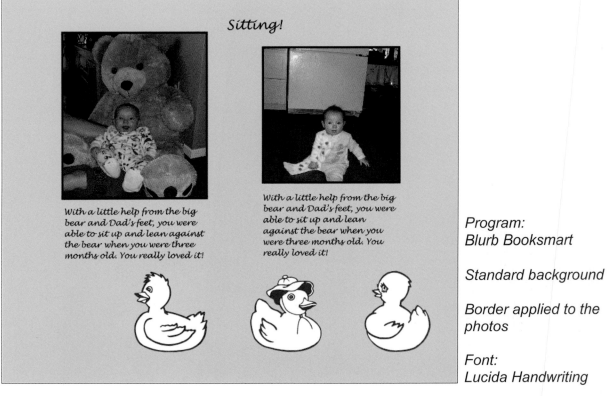

Program:
Blurb Booksmart

Standard background

Border applied to the photos

Font:
Lucida Handwriting

☞ **Write a story about sitting**

☞ **Find one or more matching photos**

Creeping and Crawling!

When it comes to crawling, all babies are different. Some babies crawl along on their bellies, while others crawl on hands and knees or even slide along the room on their bottoms. Some babies simply skip the crawling stage and start walking right away!

You could write about:
* how did the baby move?
* did he or she actually crawl or was there another method used?
* where did the baby crawl to, the very first time?

☞ **Write a story about crawling**

☞ **Find one or more matching photos**

Program:
MyPublisher

Style Collage

Font:
Kristen ITC

Playing In the Sand!

Finally the moment comes when the baby begins to play with sand, either in the sandbox or at the beach. So much sand! Of course there are always exceptions to the rule, but most children love it. Digging holes, carefully tasting a sand cake, letting the sand fall through their fingers, some babies just can't get enough.
Write about the baby's first experiences with sand:

- when did your child or grandchild play in the sand for the first time?
- where was that? In the sandbox at home, a neighborhood playground or at the beach?
- how did he or she like it?
- which toys were his or her favorites?
- were there any other children present?

☞ **Write a story about playing in the sand**

☞ **Find one or two matching photos**

Fun in the sand!

As soon as we reached the beach and the park, you could not stay away from the sand. Having fun with your shovel, and destroying your sister's castles, of course!

Program:
Picaboo

Theme Petting Zoo

Added shapes

Font:
HocKey is Life

Spending the Night

Many grandfathers, grandmothers, uncles and aunts look forward to the time they are called upon to do some babysitting. Perhaps this was the baby's first night out and the brand-new parents had a chance to have a nice quiet evening together, for the first time since the baby was born.

You could write about:
- when did the baby first stay over at someone else's house?
- with whom?
- what was the reason for this?
- how did it go? For the baby, and for Mom and Dad?
-

Spending the night

After two months you were allowed to spend a night at your grandparents'. Naturally, Grandma and Grandpa would have had you stay over much sooner, but Mum was not ready for this yet.

Grandpa and Grandma were left with a long list of instructions for feeding, changing diapers and letting you burp. You were fast asleep. Mum and Dad went to a feast at their old school.

Everything went perfect only, when Mum decided to pick up her baby again at eight o'clock, everybody was still fast asleep.

Program:
Mixbook

Background color chosen from the photo

Theme Born To Be Wild

Font:
Sensation (title)
Chaparrel Pro (text)

☞ **Write a story about the first night at somebody else's house and collect matching photos**

The Christening

If the baby has been christened, this event should be remembered in your book. For instance, describe:
- when was he or she christened?
- in which church did the christening take place?
- who led the service?
- who are the godparents?
- who else was there?
- can you tell anything special about the service?
- was there a party afterwards?

☞ **Write a story about the christening**

☞ **Find one or two matching photos**

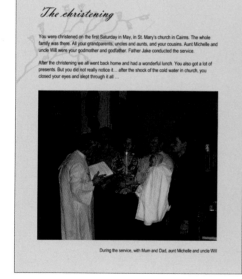

Program:
Blurb Booksmart

Standard background

Font:
Vladimir Script (title)
Arial Narrow (text)

Your Favorite Cuddly Toy

Many babies will receive an abundance of cuddly, soft animal toys. Often enough a baby will develop an affection for one particular item. This may occur already in the first year, but the child may show this favoritism to a particular toy or other item for years to come. You can write about that:

- what was the baby's favorite cuddly toy?
- who gave it to him or her?
- what was the cuddly toy called?
- did the baby ever lose the toy?

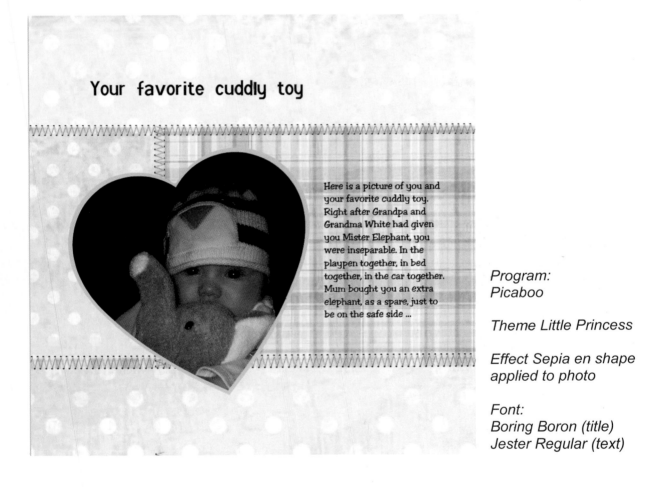

Your favorite cuddly toy

Here is a picture of you and your favorite cuddly toy. Right after Grandpa and Grandma White had given you Mister Elephant, you were inseparable. In the playpen together, in bed together, in the car together. Mum bought you an extra elephant, as a spare, just to be on the safe side ...

Program:
Picaboo

Theme Little Princess

Effect Sepia en shape applied to photo

Font:
Boring Boron (title)
Jester Regular (text)

☞ **Write a story about the favorite cuddly toy and find one or more matching photos**

Your First Favorite Toy

Most babies will also be overwhelmed with other types of toys. Sometimes, the boxes and wrappings of the toys are even more interesting than the toys themselves. The toy might be an instant success and the child plays with it for hours. But other times, a toy may be discarded after just one session of playing and never looked at again.

You can describe the following things:
- what was his or her favorite toy?
- what could you do with this toy?
- who gave this toy to him or her?

Program:
MyPublisher

Own photo as a background, 30% transparency

Font:
Jokerman (title)
DokChampa (text)

☞ **Write a story about the favorite toy and collect matching photos**

Your Best Friend

Mom and Dad are always number one, of course. But apart from them, baby might have other favorite persons. Is she always trying to hug Grandma? Or is he immediately excited as soon as Grandpa taps the window? For instance, write about:
- who is the baby's favorite person?
- how does this show?

Your best friend

Right from the start your big sister Karin was your best friend!

Program: Mixbook

Added Recommended Stickers

Font: Chaparrel Pro

☞ **Write a story about the baby's best friend and collect matching photos**

Your First Birthday

What a Lot of Presents!

Cake!

You can end the story of the baby's first year by telling about his or her first birthday party. Here are some topics you can write about:

- was the room decorated?
- how did the baby react to all the decorations?
- who came to the party?
- which presents did he or she get?
- what was the favorite present? Who gave it?
- what kind of cake was there? Is there a special story about the cake? About the frosting or how it is decorated, or about the person who baked the cake?

☞ **Write a story about the first birthday party and collect matching photos**

Program: Shutterfly | Style Year of Us | Sticker added | Font: Copperplate (title) Coquette (text)

10.3 Your Own Photo Book

Hopefully, the examples in this chapter have provided enough inspiration for you to write your own story. You can elaborate as much as you want and use as many pages as you want to tell the story of the baby's first year:

- you can leave out the titles that do not apply to your own story, and
- you can add extra titles for other topics or events.

It is up to you how much text you add to each page. You can confine yourself to writing simple captions that go with the photos, or you can fill an entire page with text. In this respect, the album software does not impose any restrictions.

 Tip

Read back
Take time once in a while to read over what you have written. You may decide to rephrase an item here and there or add extra lines to your story.

Finally, if you are satisfied with the contents of your book, you can send it to the print service and pay for it. In *Chapter 3 Working with Mixbook* you can read how to do this.

10.4 Visual Steps Website and Newsletter

So you have noticed that the Visual Steps-method is a great method to gather knowledge quickly and efficiently. All the books published by Visual Steps have been written according to this method. There are quite a lot of books available, on different subjects. For instance about *Windows*, photo editing, and about free programs, such as *Google Earth* and *Skype*.

Website
Use the blue *Catalog* button on the **www.visualsteps.com** website to read an extensive description of all available Visual Steps titles, including the full table of contents and part of a chapter (as a PDF file). In this way you can find out if the book is what you expected.

This instructive website also contains:
- free computer booklets and informative guides (PDF files) on a range of subjects;
- free computer tips, described according to the Visual Steps method;
- a large number of frequently asked questions and their answers;
- information on the free *Computer certificate* you can obtain on the online test website **www.ccforseniors.com**;
- free 'Notify me' e-mail service: receive an e-mail when book of interest are published.

Visual Steps Newsletter
Do you want to keep yourself informed of all Visual Steps publications? Then subscribe (no strings attached) to the free Visual Steps Newsletter, which is sent by e-mail.

This Newsletter is issued once a month and provides you with information on:
- the latest titles, as well as older books;
- special offers and discounts;
- new, free computer booklets and guides.

As a subscriber to the Visual Steps Newsletter you have direct access to the free booklets and guides, at **www.visualsteps.com/info_downloads**

Appendices

A. How Do I Do That Again?

In this book actions are marked with footsteps: 🐾1
Find the corresponding number in the appendix below to see how to execute a specific operation.

7 Change font size
In Wordpad:

● Click

● Click the preferred size

In Mixbook:

● Click

● Drag the scroll bar 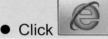 to the preferred size

8 Open the *Mixbook* window

● Click on the taskbar

9 Change text color

● Select the text

● Click

● Click the preferred color

10 Make text bold/italic

● Click **B** and/or *I*

11 Flip to a page

● Click the preferred page

12 Ad new pages

● Click Add Blank Page

13 Move page

● Drag the page to the preferred place

14 Sign in at *Mixbook*

● Click Login

● By **Email Address:**, type your e-mail address

● By **Password:**, type your password

● Click Login to Mixbook

B. Opening the Bonus Online Chapter

This is how you open the bonus online chapter on this book's website:

☞ **Open** *Internet Explorer* 👣¹

☞ **Go to the www.visualsteps.com/photobook webpage** 👣²

You will see the website that goes with this book:

⤵ **Click**
Bonus Online Chapters

Now you will see this webpage:

To open the bonus chapter:

⤵ **Click**
Start downloading »»

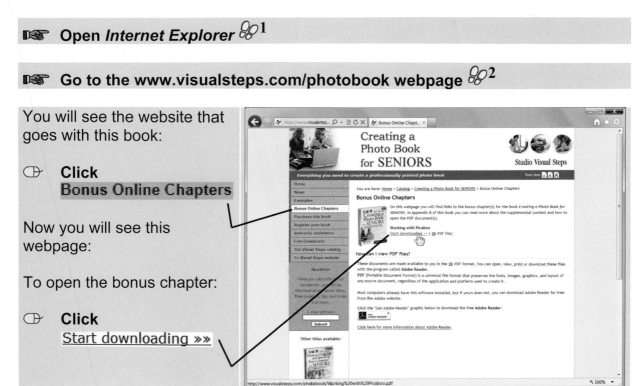

You can use the free *Adobe Reader* program to open these PDF files. This program allows you to view the files and even print them, if you wish.
The PDF files are secured by a password. To open the PDF files, you need to enter the password:

⌨ **Type:** 82431

⤵ **Click** OK

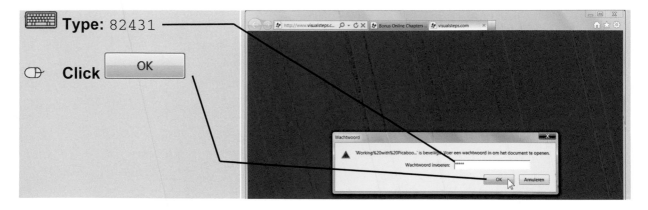

Now you will see the Bonus Chapter:

You can view this document by using the scroll bars:

You can print the document as well. Click the 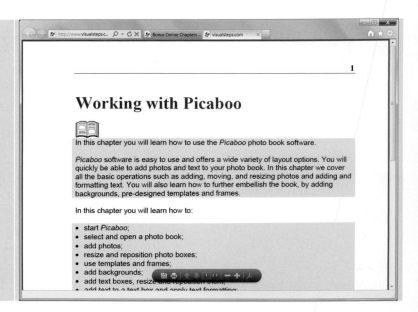 button to print the document:

You can work through this online chapter in the same way you have worked with the chapters in the book. After you have read or printed the chapter, you can close the window.

☞ **Close all windows** ℰℰ³

C. Index

Picasa for SENIORS

Picasa for SENIORS
Get Acquainted with Picasa: Free, Easy-to-Use Photo Editing Software

Author: Studio Visual Steps
ISBN: 978 90 5905 246 8
Book type: Paperback
Number of pages: 264
Accompanying website:
www.visualsteps.com/picasa

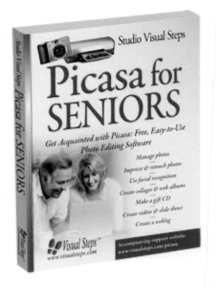

Are you looking for a handy and free photo management program? In that case the popular *Picasa* is an excellent choice! *Picasa* offers extended functionality for organizing and presenting your photo collection. It also offers several useful editing options. With just a few mouse clicks you can improve color quality and remove undesirable "red eyes". You can crop or straighten photos in a few seconds, print them or create a slide show. In order to safeguard your photos you can burn them to a CD or DVD. You can make internet web albums or publish your photos to your own blog. In other words, Picasa offers exactly what you are looking for: an easy way to manage, edit and present your photo collection.

Characteristics of this book:
- practical, useful topics
- geared towards the needs of the self-employed, independent contractor or freelancer
- clear instructions that anyone can follow
- handy, ready-made templates available on this website

You will learn how to:
- manage photos
- improve and retouch photos
- create collages and web albums
- make a gift CD
- create videos and slide shows
- create a blog

iPad for SENIORS

iPad for SENIORS
Get started quickly with the user friendly iPad

Author: Studio Visual Steps
ISBN: 978 90 5905 108 9
Book type: Paperback
Number of pages: 296
Accompanying website:
www.visualsteps.com/ipad

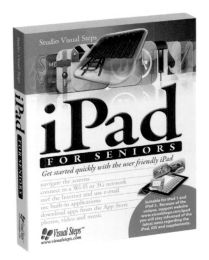

This comprehensive and invaluable guide will show you how to get the most out of your iPad. The iPad is a very user friendly, portable multimedia device with endless capabilities. Use it to surf the Internet, write e-mails, jot down notes and maintain your calendar.

But that is not all you can do with the iPad by far. With the Apple App Store you can choose from hundreds of thousands of applications (apps). Many apps can be downloaded for free or cost practically nothing. This practical tablet computer offers apps to allow you to listen to music, take and view photos and make video calls. Perhaps you are interested in new recipes, horoscopes, fitness exercises, news from around the world or podcasts? You can even use it to view the place where you live in Google Street View. There is literally an app to do almost anything.

With *iPAD FOR SENIORS* you can learn how to take complete advantage of this technology. Before you know it, you won't believe you ever lived without an iPad and your world will open up and become a lot bigger!

You will learn how to:
- navigate the screens
- connect to a Wi-Fi or 3G network
- surf the Internet and use e-mail
- use built-in applications
- download apps from the App Store
- work with photos, video and music

Photo and Video Editing for SENIORS

Photo and Video Editing for SENIORS
Create fantastic movie and photo projects!

Author: Studio Visual Steps
ISBN 978 90 5905 167 6
Book type: Paperback
Nr of pages: 408 pages
Accompanying website:
www.visualsteps.com/photovideoediting

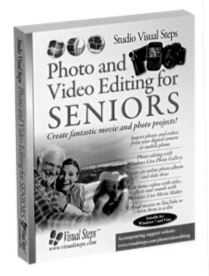

Windows Live Photo Gallery and *Movie Maker* are free programs that will allow you to organize, edit and share your digital photos and videos.
With just a few mouse-clicks you can create beautiful pictures, by editing them in the user-friendly *Windows Live Photo Gallery* program. You can share your photos with others, for instance in an online photo album, or slide show. In *Windows Live Photo Gallery* you can also easily arrange your pictures and add tags to them.
With *Windows Live Movie Maker* you can create a professional-looking movie with your videos and photos from your (grand)children, a vacation, a recent day trip or a wedding. You can add special effects, transitions, sound, and captions to your movie. To be able to show your movie to other people, you will learn how to prepare it and send it by e-mail, burn it to a DVD, or upload it to *YouTube*. Finally, we will discuss how to import your videos and photos from a digital video camera, photo camera, mobile phone or other external storage device.

You will learn how to:
- Download and install *Windows Live Photo Gallery* and *Windows Live Movie Maker*
- Arrange and edit photos
- Print and e-mail photos
- Create an online photo album
- Create a movie with *Windows Live Movie Maker*
- Add effects, music, titles and captions
- Publish your movie on *YouTube* or copy it to a DVD
- Import photos and videos from a photo camera, video camera or mobile phone